Benwell Remembered

by Yvonne Young

An aerial view of Benwell streets.

Previous page: Clara Street, Benwell, in 1967.

First published in 2009 by

Summerhill Books
PO Box 1210
Newcastle-upon-Tyne
NE99 4AH

Email: andrew_clark@hotmail.co.uk

ISBN: 978-1-906721-19-0

Contents

Introduction

I was born in Maria Street in 1952, at the time I didn't realise that we were classed as "Poor" but on looking back that was what we were, but in no way did it affect the good times we had, the community spirit and the friendships which continue to this day. Many of the old pals still meet up once a year at a reunion which is held at the West Denton Fire Station club room usually in October or November. Although I haven't lived here since 1973 when I was married, I still look back on my childhood in Benwell as the reason why I am always interested in finding out about new things and a need to recreate that close knit atmosphere around me.

For the past year I have been a member of the West Newcastle Picture History Collection group, we ensure that archive photos and maps of our area are preserved and logged for future generations to be able to view them. At first we met in the old Carnegie Library on Atkinson Road, which is where I met Andrew Clark, who was collecting photos from the archive for his book All the Lads and Lasses. I mentioned to him that I had always wanted to write about Benwell folk and their memories. He simply said: "Right then, why don't you. I'll meet you here next week to talk about it?"

I began by talking to a couple of friends who dug deep into their lofts, and they came up with the most amazing photos including street scenes from the 1950s and '60s, pubs, clubs and buildings which are all now long gone, coronation and victory tea parties from 1945. The well known local photographer, Jimmy Forsyth knew instinctively that if he didn't capture scenes just like these, that they would be lost to future generations – the iconic views down Clara Street towards the power station across the river, people going about their everyday lives and the generations that grew up there. I have realised that the memories of the folks that were around during that time can't be lost either.

This project has become a great interest of mine, and I feel that even when the book is completed, that I will still carry on talking to people from the area.

Over the past couple of months I have spoken to some strong and fascinating characters, the eldest being born in 1916 in Colston Street, and all of them agree on one thing, that Benwell was the best place to be. Everyone knew everyone else and although it's a cliche, 'the doors were left unlocked' – we didn't have anything to pinch but we didn't know that we were poor because we were rich in friendships. John Reid summed it all up when he said: "The only time we were stuck up was when we were wallpapering."

Above: The Carnegie Library which was known locally as Benwell Library on Atkinson Road, built in 1908. Pupils at my school were taken once a month to choose a book.

Left: Andrew Clark, publisher for Summerhill Books, Mike Young. Harry Bennett and Fred Millican, members of the West Newcastle Picture History Collection group at the West End Library, Condercum Road.

It's not only the recollections of times gone by that are important, but also the accounts of people who are working and living in Benwell today. The history group meet from 9-12 every Monday in West End Library. The new building is on the site of the old Majestic Cinema on Condercum Road and anyone can drop in to look at old photos, share a memory or two and point out on the map where they were then.

The West End Customer Service Centre and Library on Condercum Road.

When the old Carnegie Library building closed last year, we feared that it would fall into disrepair and, like so many beautiful buildings, that it would close down. However, thankfully the Riverside Community Health Project has expanded into the old rooms. Riverside is accommodating the recently closed Dolphin Street Centre and they continue to support activities, creche, outreach work and promote well-being for local residents and families.

Sadly Jimmy Forsyth died this year in 2009, but his legacy will live on. The documentary film *No Fancy Shades* captures the life and times of the man. He can be seen in the closing moments walking under the old railway bridge at the end of Scotswood Road whistling the Blaydon Races. A true adopted Geordie.

Right: In the West End Library with friends sharing a cup of tea, mince pie and choosing a book. Lorna Henwood is second left and Mary Butler right. Lorna was featured as a baby in the photograph below from the book 'All the Lads and Lasses'.

Left: A year after the end of the First World War there were events such as this Peace Tea in Maughan Street, Benwell in 1919.

Family Life

I was born at 17 Maria Street in South Benwell in February 1952, most people pronounced it as in Black Maria, not as in the girl's name. Our side of the street had remained untouched by the German bombs during the war, but directly opposite our house lay the waste ground which was a reminder of where houses had once stood. At the bottom of the street were the premises of the St John Ambulance Brigade, their vehicles were kept there. Further along was where the old fire station used to be.

No 17 was a downstairs flat with one bedroom, scullery and sitting room. The black leaded range oven come fireplace was in the main room. I once washed a plastic doll, opened the heavy door and placed it inside to dry. When I opened it some time later, all that was left were the eyeballs among a gooey mass. I shut the door and left it, mam said that it had been a chisel job to remove it. Lino was used and a rug placed in the centre, very few owned vacuum cleaners so the rug would be taken outdoors, hung on the line and then beaten within an inch of its life. The scullery was a Spartan affair, ceramic sink, wooden draining board with a wire across the front and a piece of cotton fabric threaded through to hide the old pans behind.

The top half of Maria Street. This photo was taken in 1987. Flats on the bottom section past Buddle Road, which has long been demolished, all had tiny garden areas surrounded by railings. The railings were taken out during the Second World War to support the war effort.

According to mam, my nana, dad's mother lived at no 17 first and they moved in with her after they were married. She used to go to St Aidan's Church which was on St John's Road. My grandfather, Charles Reginald Luscombe, had died in 1940, long before I was born. He was a mariner and sailed from Falmouth before he moved to Newcastle. My uncle Tommy, dad's brother, recalls how he used to make fishing nets in the back yard to raise extra money, he rigged a bracket on the wall to weave the rope through. Later in his life, he painted ships at Vickers Armstrong's.

My grandmother Mary Ann Luscombe holding her daughter, my aunt Beatrice, with Norman, aged about four years old.

My dad, Ken Luscombe, was born in 1920. There were eight children – George was the eldest who would become a soldier in the Northumberland Fusiliers, Alfie died during service in the army in India from TB, my dad served in Hanover, and worked in a garage on his return from service. Tommy was in a motorbike corps and now lives in Walker. He returned from the war to become a shipwright at Swan Hunter's Neptune Yard and still delivers the Herald and Post in his area in his 80s. Doris died aged 23, Margaret was only fourteen months when she died and Beatrice married James Aisbitt, had two sons, but sadly James was killed also during the war. Norman served with the Pioneer Corps and Charles wasn't in good health, he was in and out of hospital all of his life.

Mam was born Doreen Rome in Fleming Street, Gateshead in 1931. She was one of five children –

Ellen, the youngest is still living in Felling. She worked in various factories when young including Osram Lamps. John worked as a railway track worker. Leslie served in Egypt during the war and later worked for Huwood's on the Team Valley Trading Estate. Billy was a glass blower by trade. My grandad, William Rome, served in the navy, was a flyweight boxer who won many cups fighting matches in Cumbria where his family came from. He also worked as a fire fighter in Gateshead.

I remember that the Rome men were very keen on 'Backing a horse'. When the race was on TV they'd sit glued to the screen while Billy paced back and forth shouting and egging his horse on. The others would be shouting to tell him to move out of the way. When they lost, they would go over the race details or discuss 'Score draws'. Then they would fill in the pools slips, putting crosses here and there. I never understood what they were doing or saying, but would be told to "Shush" when words such as Aberdeen 0 Dunfermline 2 could be heard. There'd always be a scuffle when the newspaper was delivered. John was much smaller than Billy, but he'd give as good as he got, then he would really flip when Billy put his hand on John's head at arms length to keep him at bay. They looked just like a pair of characters from a Beano comic.

Ken and Doreen Luscombe on their wedding day in 1951. They moved in to 17 Maria Street with Ken's mother Mary Ann.

Dad met mam at a dance in town in 1950. They had a short courtship and I still have the receipt for her wedding ring – dad kept everything! We still have the letters he received from pals after demob and photos, soldier's pay book etc. He was eleven years older than her and their interests were as varied as they could be. They both enjoyed dancing, but that's where it ended. He enjoyed going for long walks, riding his pushbike, fishing and classical music. She enjoyed sun bathing, fashion and pop music. Pagliacci would play when dad was in and Elvis, Kathy Kirby or Bill Hayley when mam was at home. He also enjoyed swimming at Scotswood Baths. He'd take me with him and taught me how to swim. When we came out he'd towel dry my hair on the way to the park. We always stopped at a local shop for a box of Quality Street, I always got the nut ones, my favourites. He sometimes took a bag of hazelnuts and his nut cracker. I loved to watch as he cracked the shells, then he'd pop them one by one into my mouth. He always kept a fruit bowl full at home. If he brought an apple with him, he could snap it clean in two by pushing both thumbs into the top then prizing it apart – we would have half each. There was one other bowl, glass which was full of 'Odds and ends'. Most houses kept one of these, not always a bowl, an old tea caddy or biscuit tin would do. There would be everything in there from buttons to puncture repair kit. I loved to rummage through it.

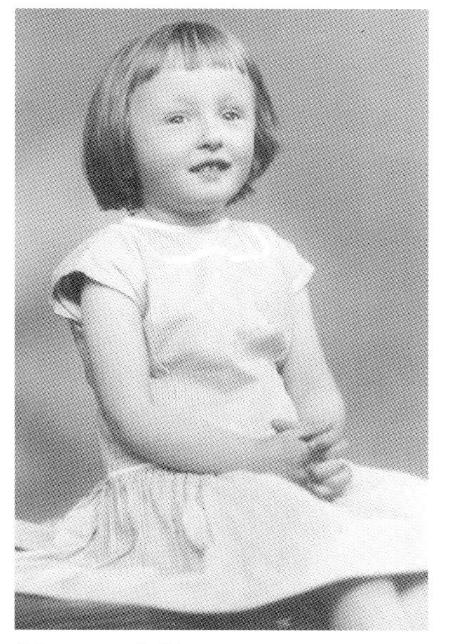
Me, aged five.

Evidence of mam's poor memory was ever present. I can recall how she was running up the street, late for work as usual, and the window cleaner running after her shouting "Wait!". She ran on shouting back "I haven't got time to pay you. I'll give you the money next time." He continued chasing her and, when he caught up, he removed a cleaning ticket from the back of her coat. She always took care of her skin using Nivea on her face morning and night. She'd put a dab on each cheek, her nose, chin and three along her forehead then rub it in, well, when she remembered. I once saw her at the bottom of the stairs ready to drag the front door open, in a hurry as usual, with all dollops still in place. When I drew her attention to this she rubbed it all in quickly then dashed out. However, on one occasion, I had been sent to the Co-op on Buddle Road for some cheese when the assistant told me that mam had been standing in the queue waiting to be served with cream all over her face, much to the hilarity of staff and customers. People would say "There's Doreen, she's dead scatty." But she did have one good tip which I carry out to this day. Before I was given a ten bob note, twenty shilling note or very rarely a fiver to go to the shops with, she would look at the note, say out loud the first two numbers and letters from the serial number, then tell me what she wanted. Even now, at 57 years of age, if I'm about to hand the assistant a note I memorise those numbers. Funnily enough, I have never needed to challenge anyone for short changing me.

My mam sitting on the steps leading up to 22 Buddle Road.

Mam's concentration span was that of a gnat, whereas dad could focus on things for hours. Dad made me a bogey from four pram wheels, knocked a couple of planks of wood together with a swivel piece at the bottom with rope attached so that I could 'Coin the corners'. The seating position was created from an orange box. It was the envy of all around, kids queued up to have a turn. One lad took too much of a liking to it and did off with it after his go. He was identified quickly and dad went up to the school. The lad was told off in front of the whole school in assembly.

On Sunday, I looked forward to listening to *Pick of the Pops* on the radio – Alan Freeman greeting us with "Hello pop pickers". When it finished *Sing Something Simple* came on and I used to rush to the radio to switch it off – that programme was for the old people. Then I ran outside to look for my pals. My life revolved around the streets, we had transistor radios which we held to our ears as we walked around. The first record I bought was *House of the Rising Sun* by the Animals.

Mr Billy Laws, the Provi man, used to knock on everyone's doors with his book and cash bag waiting for payment. We used our cheque at places like Chesterton's on Adelaide Terrace, they sold mainly clothing and household goods. I remember mam took me there once to buy me something to wear and I took ages to decide because everything was so old fashioned. It was the 1960s and the shop hadn't quite cracked the swinging bit yet. So, I came out with a brown wool twin set, which I think I swapped to a friend. I do remember while I was still at Atkinson Road School when I got a lovely double breasted skirt suit, the buttons were shaped like Maltezers and there were two vents at the back. The skirt was straight with a vent and I thought that I was 'IT'. I wore that suit till it just about fell to bits, but that was what it was like back then, you had maybe one or two decent items to wear. Now, I've got so much stuff that I don't even wear and when I iron I have to scram everything in the wardrobe so tightly that it's a waste of time having ironed in the first place. I sometimes think that it's a throw back from not having much.

I still look back with fondness on the newness of it all – Ban the Bomb badges, Radio Caroline, Herman's Hermits and I'm proud to say that I was around for each and every Doctor in *Doctor Who*!

I was asked to present this bouquet of flowers to the oldest member of St Aidan's Church. I was about 11 years old at the time. Mrs Priestley, the vicar's wife is first left, then a male member of the church, I am wearing the striped dress, Mr Priestley, the elderly lady and Mr Chambers. The event took place on the stage at the east end of the church hall.

School Life

It became clear in the infants class at South Benwell that I was set to inherit my mam's bad memory. There was a playhouse in the first class room, it had no roof and three sides which were set against the wall. I played with the toy food, opened the cupboards and made full use of the dressing up clothes. At home time mam discovered that my coat was missing, she took the teacher to task, why weren't possessions looked after etc, then it was discovered that I'd left it in the playhouse.

The rooms were large with high ceilings and huge filigreed ornate roses. We were told by the teacher that fairies lived up there and that on our birthday, one of them would come out with a penny. I didn't understand that it wasn't my birthday when a lass in my class was presented with a decorated wooden cake with real candles on to blow out, then a penny put into her hand. I screamed blue murder, where was mine?

South Benwell School, the imposing building which dominated the area, in 1960.

Gladys Bonner, also in my class from 1956 recalls: "The rooms had runners on the floor and were divided by glass partitions, they were removed when we had dancing lessons and we used to float about on the oak parquet flooring wearing our knickers and no socks on. The building was made from beautiful materials, old ornate stone, welsh dressers and iron fireplaces, I hope that some of that was salvaged when they demolished it."

All of the children in my class came from the surrounding streets, so we all knew each other and our families very well. David Young, also five years old, was later to become my husband; he lived in Frank Street, two streets along from me. Gladys lived above Moore's shop which was at the junction of Maria Street and Buddle Road. At first, our mams would take us directly to school, but after a short while we used to tag on to any mother going in that direction; they became a kind of Pied Piper along Buddle Road back lane.

A range of books that I can remember from school days.

On the subject of learning, we were given Janet and John books – really middle class drawings of happy cleanly scrubbed children who played in gardens while mother collected flowers in a basket. They played with new toys and their parents spoke nicely and politely to them. The content wasn't very stimulating – we were rough and ready, streetwise kids. J and J's lifestyles were far removed from our own.

"I walked and I walked and what did I see? I saw a little puppy and he saw me. Little puppy ran, he ran to me."

"Look Mother," said Janet. "He is a dear little puppy."

Any dog in our area ran the streets without a lead.

"I shall stop and get off," said Janet. "You must have a swing next."

"Thank you," said Jill.

In contrast we had to fight our corner to get a turn on the Witch's Hat. It was very dangerous when the circular seat crashed against the iron pole in the centre, and if your fingers were in the way you knew about it. The Tea Pot Lid roundabout was much safer. Swings hadn't lasted five minutes in Buddle Road playground and I can't remember any green areas to play on.

In needlework lessons everyone had a piece of red hessian with holes in. We used embroidery cotton to create little squares to be used as bookmarks or placemats. The teacher explained that as there had been too much talking in class everyone was moving desks. The girls couldn't sit next to a friend and would be paired with a boy. David Young (later to be my husband) sat next to me and couldn't thread his needle. He continually asked me to thread it for him or remove knots.

Yvonne: "Why divn't yi use shorter lengths and then it wouldn't knot?"

David: "Cos it keeps comin' oot."

Yvonne: "Gis it here, aal thread it, yar nearly puttin' me eye oot."

David Young together with Angus Errington playing guitar in the back yard of Frank Street in the 1960s. Angus was more like a brother to David and came along to family outings.

David and Angus talking about old times in 2004.

South Benwell School pupils from 1931 – twenty-seven years later I started at this school.

Gladys Bonner looked forward to milk time: "The milk bottles were those wide necked kind. We used a milk bottle top opener, it was shaped like a flying saucer and you pressed it into the top to stop your fingers going into the milk."

Gladys was sent to school one day with a kidney infection: "My mam explained to the teacher that I would have to be allowed to use the toilet whenever I asked.

Gladys: "Please miss, can I leave the room?"

Teacher: "No, finish your milk."

Gladys: "Miss, I've finished my milk, can I go to the toilet now?"

Teacher: "You might as well wait until playtime, it's only half an hour away."

Gladys: "Please Miss, I can't wait."

Gladys said: "The teacher ignored me, and consequently I had an accident. She called for a dinner lady, Annie Reay to take me home. Annie offered to clean me up, but in front of the whole class the teacher said "No, she must go to her house."

Gladys (née Bonner) and Billy Campbell as they are today at their home in Fenham. Billy has his own construction company and Gladys works at a nearby school.

"When my mam found out about this she marched up to the school and demanded her resignation. There was a meeting at the Civic Centre, but by then mam had calmed down and stepped back saying: "I don't want the lass to lose her job, so I'm not taking it any further." The head teacher thanked her saying that Mrs X was a really good teacher and that she was sorry for what had happened."

A monitor would be selected to take a cup of tea to each teacher in the school. (Risk assessments weren't a requirement then, no parent would know the first thing about suing.) I was given the job one day and the two last cups of tea were designated for school secretary Mrs Clarke and top class teacher Mr Scott. The cup was on a saucer with a biscuit at the side. I took it to Mr Scott who was on yard duty. I'd negotiated about eight sets of stone stairs on the west side of the building and walked across the yard looking at the biscuit. As I handed it over, he said: "I don't eat biscuits, you have it." It was the loveliest taste. Then I went back upstairs to collect Mrs Clarke's tea. The head teacher said: "Here's Mr Scott's tea, take it to him on the yard."

Me: "But I've already given him the tea."

Head teacher: "But ... Mr Scott doesn't like biscuits!"

She gave me such a piercing, knowing look, or had I imagined it, but she would have realised immediately when I brushed my hand over my mouth. She didn't say anything, but was very agitated. She put another biscuit on the saucer and said: "Now, this time give this to Mrs Clarke, please!"

I never got the job again.

In my opinion, we hadn't learned much until Mr Scott took over. I clearly recall the first lesson. He said that he wanted to know how much we knew. He put a huge lino like map on the wall and asked us: "Does anyone know where the British Isles are?" He was shocked to find that most of us didn't know. Then he went on to point to America, China, Japan etc and hardly anyone knew these places. With exasperation he growled: "What have these people been teaching you?"

We were split into sets for the first time. Previously the desks were arranged in rows one behind the other. Desks were now arranged in groups of six and he gave out sums. We were to complete them in silence then bring them to his desk. For the first time also I knew the meaning of the red pen. We were on the verge of sitting our Eleven Plus exams and most of us were in no way prepared. Some children who had been picked out as possible high school material were given work books with a format which would be comparable with what would be given in an examination environment.

I will never forget Mr Scott's epic determination to teach us something. Before his arrival we were obviously on the scrap heap already, not worth the bother, and would have been expected to work in industry even though this had been in decline for years. "They'll not amount to much." One day he announced that we were to listen to a programme on evolution, it was a kind of play about Darwin and natural selection, you could hear a pin drop. Maybe I have this view of him being some kind of hero because I was interested in learning, but I could never master arithmetic. My heart sank before a lesson and I was lucky if I got one out of ten. English, Art and History were my favourites and I would go to the library on a regular basis out of school.

When the results came out for the Eleven Plus exams, there were options according to our marks. Rutherford was the top school, Pendower School for Girls next, John Marlay School for Boys and Atkinson Road Secondary was for those of us who didn't "Pass". One pal of mine, Kathleen Welch had a coveted place for Rutherford. She wore a smart black blazer, black skirt and white shirt with a tie. The Pendower lasses wore bowler hats. All of us kids who didn't pass were secretly jealous of them and taunted them mercilessly with: "There gan the swats," or "There gan the poshies."

One of My Poems

We were given titles for our stories such as 'The Life of a Penny' or 'A Worm's Eye View of the World'. I enjoyed writing poems, about my pet bird, games etc but I was also aware of what sort of vehicles came out of Vickers at the bottom of Scotswood Road and that countries went to war.

I wrote a poem about the tanks. I can't remember it now but I imagined three tanks coming up Clara Street, each one had the earth on top, the first was green, the second in flames and the third blackened. There were two people waiting – one standing and one seated. I wrote it in my exercise book for English lesson with Mrs Bell, she called me out to the front of the class.

"You haven't written this, you must have copied it from a book."

Much later, I explained to my brother the gist of the poem, I have no record of it, and he drew a picture using felt tipped pens. It was exactly how I imagined it would look.

My brother David Luscombe has always enjoyed painting, drawing and making 3D models. He is now self employed working on digital images and photography. This photo was taken in his room at Hampstead Road where he lived with our dad Ken.

David drew this of Vicker's and the tanks when I told him of a poem I wrote while in the top class at South Benwell. It was a worrying time for kids in the early 1960s with talk of war with Russia over the Cuba crisis.

Games

Games in the school yard were divided into those for lads and lasses and never the twain shall meet. We used a massive skipping rope so that up to ten of us could jump together, the one who caught her foot and stopped the rope, was out or had to turn the rope. The songs were always ringing out:

1, 2, 3 O'Leary
I saw me Auntie Mary
Sittin' on the lavatory
Eatin' chocolate biscuits.

All in together girls
Never mind the weather girls
Jump in when your birthday comes
January, February, March ... (Lasses jumped in until the line was full)

Kids enjoyed sitting in a circle with their feet pressed together, and each shoe the leader touched at the end of the rhyme, that person removed a foot. If they were hit twice, the leader would say: "Right, yor oot!" Then she'd restart the rhyme: "Ibble obble black bobble – Ibble obble oot."

A craze for 'Two baller' was on the go. We used two balls juggling them against a wall – the clever clogs kids used three and could juggle in the air also. Mothers were alarmed by another craze. We'd put a ball into a nylon stocking and thwack it back and forth as we stood with our backs against the wall. If we could get our hands on a piece of chalk we'd write "Follow this line" then draw a continuous line all around the play ground. At the end we'd write: "If you followed this line you are daft."

The lads played football. There'd be a leader, usually the one who owned a ball. He'd get 'Forst pick' before the leader of the opposition then both lads would take their choice of players.

Liggies (Marbles) was another schoolyard game. Kids usually kept them in their pockets but if a mam was handy with a sewing needle they'd be kept in a little bag. We girls weren't interested in this game but we'd hear the lads saying things like: "Aal swop yi ten clemmies fo ya boller". I've since learned that a boller was a ball bearing and clemmies were stones. There were other rules depending on the patterns inside the marble.

They also played conkers and they'd negotiate: "Aav got a niner, gis them three o' yours for it." This translated: "the niner had smashed nine other folks conkers." Then the object of the game was to "Knock them oot." And as the result of a poor aim, shouts of: "Ow, yi got me hand!"

Canning Street netball team of 1961

Atkinson Road Secondary Modern

David and Gladys were in my class at Atkinson Road School in 1962 but, for the first time, we were among kids from other schools and outside of our tight knit circle. Kenneth Fairbanks, who got Fairy as a nickname, wore his hair in a slick backed teddy boy style. He didn't contest the name as he was cool, like the Fonz, so what name he had didn't bother him. His pals were Colin, who was tiny like me, and Arthur Wood who was very skinny. They all had a good sense of humour and we all got on well. We were only to stay at this school for two years as the comprehensive system was about to be introduced and then we'd be split to the four winds once more.

I wasn't allowed to take woodwork or metalwork – only cookery (it was called Housecraft) and needlework were available to the girls. We were asked to buy a basket in which to carry home our creations. I bought a square wickerwork one, it had a flowery elasticated cover with a centre opening. Some of my friends had gondola baskets, I really longed for one of those, but my mam said: "I'm not forking out for another one, you'll just have to use that one until it gets tatty."

I felt really old fashioned using it, but it did finally get tatty. It used to click my knee length white socks, so she succumbed and I had my fabulous gondola. I took great pride in placing the food that I had cooked to take home. My mam loved the pasties I made but she wasn't great on the home baking, so she never asked me for the recipe and only preferred me to make them from then on in. She only ever cooked once a week for Sunday dinner – a roast chicken. Then home made rice pudding made with lots of milk, sugar and eggs. There was always a brown skin on the top and I loved waiting for the seal to be broken to reveal the lovely white rice, the smell was unbelievable. She much preferred sitting in the sun, either in the back yard on her deck chair or on one of the six crumbling steps at the front – 'Getting a tan'. She'd dismantle the pipes on the painted green iron oven, clean them, put it back together again, and it wouldn't be used again until the next Sunday.

The corner of the veranda where Mr Dewhirst's office was situated in Atkinson Road Secondary School. Compare this photo with Bob Speight's on page 43.

Left: I took this photo of Atkinson Road in 2008, the dining hall is richly decorated by the children's work. When I was there in 1963 as a pupil the hall walls were rigged up with gym bars. (Which can be seen in Bob Speight's class on page 44.) In the 1960s the domestic science room was in the far left corner leading off the main hall on the ground floor. Back in the 1960s the hall was also used as a dining hall, then everything would be cleared away for assemblies and PE lessons.

Atkinson Road Primary School in 1928. In those days the children would share their toys and perhaps the two at the front – the dog and cat – were well played with by this class.

The set up in the cookery room was, cook one week and clean the next. It was during one session I left an onion in the pan and, when I finally checked it, the whole thing had disintegrated with the base of the pan turned to solid black. I just put it back in the cupboard and couldn't be bothered to scrape it. However, at play time, my pal Katie came out into the yard fuming: "Some bugger burnt a pan and hoyed it back in the cupboard and Aa was on cleanin' the pans this week."

My pal Gladys remembered the cookery teacher, Miss Mofatt, who before a lesson she would say: "Get out your bowls and your spoons, first of all, make sure that your bowl is clean."

Gladys once attempted to make cinder toffee. The girls all had little tins waiting for the mixture to be tipped in ready for the journey home. Gladys left hers in the pan too long and it set like bell metal with the fork upright. Miss Mofatt took one look at it she said: "You'll have to take it home in the pan, and don't forget to bring the pan back."

I learned how to make Cornish Pasties, scrambled egg, coconut haystacks and scones, and always took them home. If the recipes called for more than one egg, the teacher advised us to crack each one, then smell to see if it was off. "If you put them all in together, one may be rotten and then you have spoiled you cake." She did on one occasion find a smelly egg, much to her delight, as if to illustrate her point. She sent me over to the shop, the most embarrassing experience, and when I came back she triumphantly demonstrated the cracking and sniffing of the good egg.

Gladys too always took her efforts home, her mam would say: "Ooooo Gladys, that's lovely" then when she thought she was out of earshot could be heard saying: "Quick, she's gone out, chuck it in the bin before she comes back."

One lass in our class always had the food eaten before she got home, she always got told off, but she still did it. Money was tight for most families so she knew that she wouldn't have much to eat, especially because her dad was out of work and there were five of them. If we made small cakes we sometimes used to have a taste of each others to sample the different flavours but she never shared. She used to cover her basket with her arm, then run off to a safe distance to eat it.

The teacher asked us at the end of one lesson: "Please bring for the next session, a tin of salmon, potatoes, onion and breadcrumbs." We all thought that she meant us to crumble some bread. "Oh, no ... they are bought from the shops in a container with little holes in the top to allow you to sprinkle them over the food." It was the first time we'd heard of such a thing.

Me: "Mam, I need a tin of salmon for next week for cookery."
Mam: "What does she think she's on, her granny's yacht?"
Me: "Aw mam, aa've got ti have it for the lesson, the teacher'll kill is if aa havn't gor it."

I took the salmon next lesson and discovered that some of the lasses had brought pilchards. I didn't tell mam. When I presented my mam with my masterpiece, she took the fork, dug it into the dish of fish pie and drawled: "What a waste of a tin of salmon, it's no more than a giant fish cake!" It was probably the only time I ever got to eat all of it to myself.

We were being groomed for housewifedom, I laugh out loud when I recall the Good Housekeeper style books that we were given: "Put your house in shining good order." And: "Your home should have winking bright windows and laundry fresh curtains."

She'd obviously not experienced life in Benwell in the 1960s. The houses were crumbling down around us, leaking bay windows and demolition going on everywhere. Mothers were hard pushed to keep anything clean. Even if the linen was clean when it started out on the line it was difficult to keep it that way. Washing lines were strung across the back lanes and when the coal van came along the women had to run out to raise their props. There was an awful upsurge of coal dust as the sacks hit the tarmac.

We used to enjoy a lesson in the gym; there were wooden bars from floor to ceiling on which we could hang upside down. I hated the ropes with alternate knots. We were meant to shin down them, but I always slid burning my hands. The box and the buck were my favourites. We used to take a run up, bounce on the springboard and pounce over the top onto these old mats. One lesson I remember a lad in our class took the top from the box, hid inside, replaced the lid and stayed there for the whole of the lesson. He wasn't missed by the teacher. When we finally got new mats, everyone was very excited to try them. They were blue plastic covered sponge with Velcro at the edges, the smell was like a new inner tube on a bike. We couldn't believe how comfortable the landings were after leaping from the equipment. The older kids had the hall for the next lesson while I was on an errand to the headmaster's office and, as I looked down from the balcony, there was a lad called John ensconced inside a mat which he had fastened around himself using the Velcro – all that was visible were his head and feet. He shuffled along, penguin style shouting: "I am a Dalek."

Just then Mr Dewhirst, the head came bursting out from his office. "You boy, you stupid boy, get out of that mat immediately and get up here to see me!"

John got such a shock he fell over, hit the floor like a felled tree and was trapped in his "Dalek" shouting for his friends to get him out. It was the most entertaining errand I ever ran.

Atkinson Road School camping trip of 1963. Stuart Talbot is in the second row from back, third from right. Robert Evans (known as Nev) is in the front row, right.

In the school yard, during the 1960s, the lasses started to customise their clothes to be fashionable. The Beatles had just been discovered and I remember one lass who had written 'THE BEETLES' on the back of her jumper in large letters, then scribbled an A over the top of the second E. The older lasses still tatted their hair and often had competitions in the yard for who could back comb the fastest before the bell went. Playtimes were very much a social event. We played jacks with small metal sputnik objects and a bouncy ball. We did win each other's jacks, but always gave them back at the end of a game. Skippys was popular, and we all joined in. We had carried our friendships from South Benwell to Atkinson Road, but the Comprehensive System was looming large and our tight knit community was to be split. It was the beginning of what had already started during the demolition of housing in the area.

Pupils of Atkinson Road School taken in the yard in 1960.

Benwell Comprehensive School

The lads were packed off to John Marlay Boys School and the girls to Pendower Girls School (the name was changed to Benwell School).

We were resented from the start at this school as the established pupils, who had all passed their Eleven Plus, were highly annoyed to be sharing their environment with us, the rejects. To further set us apart, we wore pinafores with either pink or blue dog toothed check shirts while "they" were allowed to continue wearing their white shirts and ties. Thankfully they no longer wore their bowler hats or there would have been bullying beyond belief. Girls came from other schools such as Canning Street, Elswick etc and there were major adjustments to be made by us all, teachers included.

At first we were split into new letter streams, 3M1, 3M2, 3M3 for our year, the older girls were in 4M groups. After 3 months we took the same tests as the higher P and R classes, although they had studied there for the past 2 years, to decide which class we would go into next. I took to the lessons here like a duck to water, still couldn't manage maths, but I came second throughout my whole year group, including the grammar pupils, so I was moved into a P class. *Macbeth* was one of the first plays we studied – they used an old Dansette record player, it was brown and cream. We covered poets I hadn't heard of and I loved history and biology. Although I wasn't religious, I enjoyed RE, the teacher had a secular bias and the lessons were centred around discussing fact against fiction. Mrs Appleby continued to encourage me throughout my time at the school. Miss Cubitt was a fantastic English teacher, she always made the lessons fun and interesting, she'd sweep into the room and address us: "Good morning ladies." When I compare the titles of The Life of a Penny for an essay, to the topics we covered in her class, there was no comparison. She would bring a wine bottle, hold it up to the light, then describe to us how it looked to her, the rainbow colours, who had used it, what the contents had tasted of – she was an inspiration.

I was taken to one side after a biology lesson by one teacher and she commented that I was wearing nail varnish. Kindly she explained to me that this was not allowed and that she had a jar of acetone in the cupboard which would remove it. She went on to say that acetone was in all nail varnish remover preparations which were sold in the shops. This attitude totally amazed me, I wasn't greeted with a telling off in front of the class as would have been the case at Atkinson Road, instead I actually learned something. Now that's what I call a teacher, someone who can turn a possible confrontation into a lesson. Once inside the walk-in cupboard, I was overawed to see dozens of huge old Victorian glass jars with huge stoppers in the top. It took both hands to remove one from the shelf. She tipped it to soak some of the liquid onto a cloth, and the offending nails were cleaned up. (Years later when I had left the school it was reported that the bomb disposal squad were called to the school to remove these highly toxic and dangerous bottles.)

Irene Jacques wearing the Benwell Comprehensive School uniform.

I really enjoyed Biology lessons at first and learning about the ear, teeth, the heart, but then we were expected to dissect worms. During one such lesson, formaldehyde aroma and the sight of a worms innards didn't appeal to me, but when the teacher mentioned: "Look at how sharp the scalpels are, they are used for lancing veins," I slid from the high stool in the lab right onto the concrete floor. Everyone flew into a panic and a wheelchair was used to drive me to the nurse's room. I also fainted once in the art class. We were using tools to gouge lines in those clay coloured tiles and they smelled of old tyres. The teacher demonstrated safe use of the equipment: "Now be careful girls, these tools are very sharp and be sure to hold the tile away from the direction of the blade."

Someone didn't listen to the good advice and gouged a chunk from the soft area between her thumb and forefinger. Needless to say I fainted, adding to the commotion of screams and blood everywhere. Who'd be a teacher?

Sometimes during an art lesson we'd be taken with our boards, paper and pens into the tree covered outdoor area to draw the foliage around us. I loved times like this and always made really detailed sketches.

Before lessons, there was always time to discuss what we had watched on TV the night before. The most popular show was *The Man from UNCLE*. The girls used to swoon over pictures from the *Jackie* magazine of the two secret agents from the show and you either liked David McCallum or Robert Vaughan. I liked neither, but I pretended that I liked the younger one, just to fit in to the discussion. I really preferred to watch comedies such as *Not Only But Also* with Peter Cooke and Dudley Moore or radio shows such as *The Huggets* and *The Navy Lark* with Jon Pertwee.

Playtimes in the school yard were completely different from those at Akky Road. The girls played tennis and spoke of backhand and slams and 30 love – all of which was alien to us. We stuck to our games of rounders and skippys. They even used playtimes to catch up with singing lessons and making costume dolls in beautiful golden fabrics. But I did make strong friendships with some of the lasses there and appreciate now how we were given the chance to extend our education, even thought most of us didn't take up the opportunities on offer. In later life I recalled those lessons and did eventually go back to evening classes to pick up where I had left off.

Canning Street School

A Canning Street School trip in 1948 to the Hadrian's Wall. The teacher is Mrs Levy. The donor of the photograph was Miss S. Yellow, a teacher at the school.

Canning Street pupils on a school outing in 1948.

Canning Street pupils in 1948. Another photograph by Miss Yellow.

Good Friday

Men holding the Sunday School banner aloft as they proceed among the crowds out in force on this day through Canning Street.

Benwell and District Sunday Schools

44th ANNUAL
GOOD FRIDAY
Demonstration
1955

PLACE OF MEETING
Foot of Condercum Road, (Majestic Cinema) 9-30 a.m.

ROUTE :—
Condercum Road, Atkinson Road, Buddle Road, (stop & sing) Maria Street, Armstrong Road, Clara Street, (stop & sing), Ash Street, Barnesbury Road, Ladykirk Road, Glebe Street, Strathmore Crescent, (stop & sing), Colston Street, finish at Condercum Road, (Majestic Cinema)

ORDER OF PROCESSION

Westgate Hall Silver Prize Band

1	Paradise Methodist	Pink
2	Benwell Grove Methodist	Lavender
3	Bond Memorial Methodist	Green
4	Newcastle City Mission (Sopwith St.)	Red
	Boy's Brigade Band	
	Newcastle City Mission (Atkinson Rd.)	Red
5	Benwell Presbyterian	White
	Boy's Brigade Band	
6	Benwell Baptist	Blue

OFFICIALS

President and Chairman Rev. R. J. Doidge, B.Sc., (Paradise)
Speakers: Rev. R. J. Doidge, Rev. Rufus Booth, Mr. R. W. Sargent, Mr. J. H. D. Walton, B.Sc., Mr. Halcrow.
Secretary Mr. S. W. Starkey. *Treasurer* Mr. A. Wilson
Chief Marshall Mr. A. Wilson

The church programme shows the order of the day's singing schedule. It is dated 1955.

A large crowd in Colston Street in the 1960s.

Right: Parishioners stop and sing in Gerald Street. The photo was taken in 1983. Christine Wood can be seen among the crowd to the front far right, holding a hymn sheet against the front of her black coat. Christine was a former pupil of Benwell Comprehensive School for Girls.

Working Folks

Making ends meet was the deciding factor which forced many into sideline jobs. Names for these folks were The Mint Lady, who came around the streets on Sundays to sell to those making Sundays dinner. The Stick Man, he chopped wood and brought it to homes for the coal fires. There were also many door to door salesmen who offered laces, polish and cloths and combs. They must have made very little, but still tried to supplement what little they had.

After the war years there were lots of men out of work. Industry had in the past supplied work for the area and it kept the community together, but the coal, leatherworks and munitions were all either finished or on the decline. Maureen Elliot lived in Maria Street with her mother Chrissie, father Reggie and brother Reggie jnr. She remembers how she was sent with a pram up the lane to a friend of the family's house. He worked for the coal board and had an allowance of coal which was dumped outside his back door in a pyramid shape. Maureen's job was to pay him for a pram full of the precious stuff, then bring it back home – times were tough. She also was sent up to a shop on the Pipe Track Lane to buy broken biscuits for the family.

Margaret Welch remembers: "There was a paper shop at the bottom of Frank Street, then Maughan Street the next one along. The London and Newcastle Tea Company was next to a pork butchers shop. We used to stand near the door and sniff and sometimes the butcher would allow us to fetch a slice of bread from home and dip it in the saveloy gravy. There was also home made pease pudding, you could get a halfpenny dip. We used to go there with a jug to buy the pea soup.

"I lived in Maughan Street in the 1930s. We weren't allowed to play in the streets and all the houses had wooden blinds. My mam used a yellow rubbing stone on the step. She used to bake pies and put a cup upside down on top of the meat to stop the top falling into the gravy, so it didn't get soggy.

"We enjoyed polling time because there would be lots of paper to be had. We used to make paper balls out of it and they had to be rolled very tight so that they were hard, then we could pelt them at people. We'd hear the MPs shouting: "Vote for so and so, they were battling it out."

Housebuilders in Ellesmere Road. This photo was taken in 1900. Most of the workers are wearing aprons and caps. Two gents are wearing bowler hats.

Mrs Wilson with daughter and son in their back yard using the poss tub.

"When my mam died, my dad had a hard time, going to work and looking after us kids. I felt sorry for him one day and I washed the scullery floor. When he came back he said: "Have you done that, good lass?"

Times were hard for Margaret. "I had half a doll – I had it one day and my sister had it the next."

"Before we went to the cinema, me and Lily would ask for sweets, our dad would say: "Mind, if you get sweets now, don't go asking for an ice cream once we're inside!"

"Then we'd be sitting when the lady came past with the ices and Lily would read out in a loud voice: "ICE CREAM" and dad would say "Look at her she's hinting."

Margaret enjoyed thinking of where the old buildings stood: "The cinema stood down from Adelaide Terrace where the old Woolworths used to be. There were the tan yards, and one little street, Paradise Street, just a row of houses. We used to go along Eveline Gardens and Scotswood Road. There used to be allotments with rhubarb, we'd pinch a couple of sticks if nobody was around."

"We used to buy halfpenny worth of black bullets, and one day I called at the shop and the box had been in the window too long in the sunlight and all of the sweets were stuck together, so the shop keeper said: "Oh, I can't be bothered with this, I can't get them apart, you can have the lot for a halfpence."

Margaret went home as happy as Larry and made herself sick by eating the lot. She now lives in Consett and her daughter Kath lives in Woodbridge, Suffolk. Kath visits Margaret at home in her cottage and she still has the dining suite that she used at Maughan Street. The leather seats are held in place by brass buttons and the workmanship on the wood is excellent.

Trevor Atkinson remembers how his mother worked hard throughout the 1950s and '60s. The family lived at No 10 Paradise Street and his mother was called Mary Elizabeth (née Richmond) but got Molly for short. "She worked at the Empire Theatre in town as an usherette so I used to get in free with my cousins Bobby, Elaine and Marilyn. I remember watching *William Tell*, the character was played by C. Phillips and the theme tune was sung by David Whitfield.

Her next job was for Stephenson's Wholesalers, the customers came in with their Provi tickets. She also spent time working in a china shop, Fisher's China and Fancy goods. She used to bring broken plates home and me and my dad used to sit gluing them together."

He also had happy memories of going to the Regency on Atkinson Road which was run by a professional dancing couple: "He was known as Uncle Billy, they charged a tanner, an old sixpence, to get in. They also ran dance classes for little 'uns. We did the Bradford Barn and The Twist. The Boys' Brigade was next door in an old hut. Further down the road was the Moorside Boys' Club – it was run by a woman called May. There were music, dancing and a tuck shop. The lasses from South Benwell School also used the building for their domestic science lessons."

Fatty the Rag Man was a popular figure in the community, he trawled the streets and back lanes once a week. Lilan Barclay remembers: "I loved to hear him blow his bugle, this was the herald to his approach. You could get a fish or a balloon. I once gave him a coat for a goldfish but it turned out that it was my mam's best one. She had to run after him to get it back – boy did I get a hiding."

The chimney sweep was always in work, and Gladys Bonner said that it seemed to her, every time her mother had decorated there would be a fall of soot from the chimney and the whole place was filthy again. When she mentioned this I recalled being fascinated by the sweep. He would unravel a huge cloth on the floor which doubled as a carrying case for his tools and a cover over the fireplace, it had a hole in the middle. There were lots of metal rods which he fixed together to make a long pole, then the circular brush was attached, and slotted through the hole in the cloth. This was the cue to run outside to watch the brush explode through the chimney. A crowd would have gathered in the lane, everybody knew the chimney sweep and were sure of a show when he entered someone's house. I never knew his name and I used to ask him lots of questions but all he ever said was "Shush". Mam laughed one day when I asked "Mam, is the sweep called Shush?"

Rag and bone man, Alan Burns, in the back lane of Maria Street and Maughan Street in 1967/68. He could be heard shouting "Rags and woollens, bring out your rags and woollens." The horse was kept in a building on Beaumont Street. The lad in the white top is called Kevin.

Buddle Road where Jackie White's fish shop stood. Dodgson's general dealer shop was next door. Jackie used to chop the fish with a huge axe and I wanted to watch, but was too small. I used to hold on to the top of the counter and climb up until he said "Don't climb up there pet." At the end of the working day, Jackie used a scrubbing brush and lots of soapy water to clean the wooden cutting bench.

Jackie White in 2009.

A photograph taken in the 1950s – to the left ahead would lead to Pipe Track Lane and Maria Street. To the right led to Maughan Street. This is Buddle Road back lane, back of Nos 112 and 114 – in the middle of that block where Jackie White's fish shop stood. When I showed Jackie this photo he said: "That's my mini and that's my daughter sitting on the path."

Henry Harrison wearing his bus conductor uniform.

Charlie Thompson and Eleanor Peddie. Charlie worked as a butler, a friend of the Kirk and Peddie families.

David Young making a telephone order at the Co-op garage where he was foreman.

Chimney sweeps of Benwell, father and son team George and Philip Bowden of Gill Street

Mrs D. Winstance and Mr A. Bell in 1964 when the cables were laid all along Buddle Road. The photo was taken looking east

Glen's Cafe was originally began in 1956 by Benny and Joyce Curry. Now their son Keith (pictured right) and wife Joan run the business.

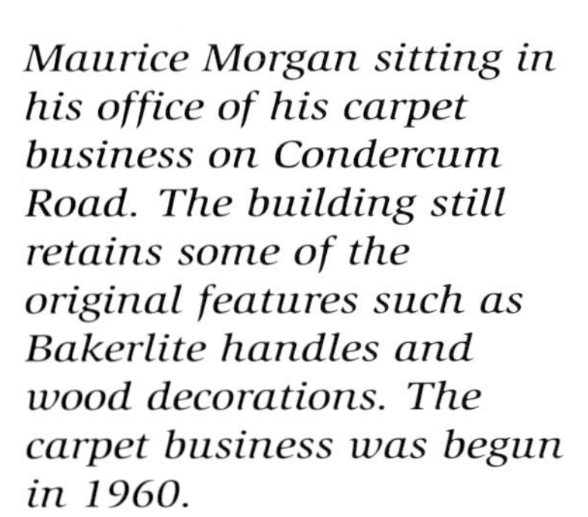

Maurice Morgan sitting in his office of his carpet business on Condercum Road. The building still retains some of the original features such as Bakerlite handles and wood decorations. The carpet business was begun in 1960.

Audrey Guthrie is a well known character in Benwell. She is a champion boxer and the first female to box in the North East to become professional. She is also a bus driver for stagecoach. She was brought up on Pendower Way. I first met her when she was about 17, she came to help out with the activities and trips at the summer playscheme I was working on.

Kevin Logan, Sabana Ahmed and Christine Irklis – some of the staff of the Riverside Community Health Project who are based in the old Benwell Library building. Anne Bonner is manager of the centre. The Dolphin Street Community Centre, run by Ron French, moved into the building in 2009.

Above: Patrick S. Ruo and above right: Heri Pinto. They are reception/security officers at the West End Customer Service Centre and Library on Condercum Road.

Right: The official opening of the West End Customer Service Centre and Library on Condercum Road on Monday February 9th 2009. Staff and guests enjoy a buffet in the functions room.

John Shaxon, on Condercum Road, he has been a lollipop man for around fifteen years.

Christine Wood, librarian at the West End Library on Condercum Road stares in awe at the hand embroidered bedspread which took Sylvia Wood (Of Woolly West fame) three years to complete. The work is embellished in highly coloured threads showing butterflies and flowers. When the quilt is turned onto the opposite side, the stitches are just as neat.

Mr Barndrres behind the counter of his shop on Atkinson Road, he has owned this business for 29 years.

Heather McLeod, receptionist to Thompson's Opticians in the shopping precinct on Adelaide Terrace.

Search Project staff on Adelaide Terrace – Maggie Crane, Jacqueline Metcalf and Dee Johnson.

The Adelaide Café, in May 2009, where customers can enjoy anything from a toastie to a full English breakfast or roast dinner and lovely puddings. The photo shows the then owners behind the counter Kelly (née Scott) Graham and husband Chris Graham. Kelly's mam Lynn Rushforth is standing at the front. New owners took over in September 2009.

Mick the Fish fruiterers and fresh fish shop. Workers Gary Hall and Debbie Johnson pictured outside.

Gillian Fradgley at Leveys paint and decorating supplies shop on Adelaide Terrace. Gillian formerly lived at 123 Buddle Road in the 1960s and '70s.

Street Life and Social Life

We were never in the house if we could help it, there was always someone outside to play a game with. We had tops and whips. The string on the whip was bound tightly around the top then we had to kneel on it, pull the whip so that the top went spinning along the concrete path. The lasses used chalks to decorate the plain light wood. There was a metal tip at the end which got hot after spinning and it was used to burn someone on the arm "For a laugh". Wrist burns were also popular to win an argument.

The metal railings had been removed from the walls outside the houses during the war years to add to the supply of metal for armaments. This gave free range for a game called "Running the walls". You'd start off at the top of the street, jump the first wall and pick up speed like a hurdler until you got to the bottom of Scotswood Road.

Clara Street in 1967 where we would 'run the walls'.

Houses were crumbling around us and this suited us kids just fine. We had an adventure playground with no restrictions of risk assessments as there are today, no cordoned off areas. All we needed was a collection of near perfect old bricks to construct our own little four walls, decorate it with bits of broken glass and tins. On occasion there'd be the odd oil container, battery acid or broken pipes as a bonus.

Treats which could be bought from Mr Cook's shop at the corner of Edgeware Road and St. John's Road. Coins we used to use, the threepenny bit, farthing, halfpennies and pennies. (The coin we know as 5 pence was once known as a tanner or sixpence, its worth around two and a half pence today.)

On the top corner of Edgeware Road and St John's Road stood Mr Cook's shop. He was ahead of his time in the early 1960s as he placed chocolate bars in the freezer on lolly sticks. Now, the kids take frozen Marathons etc for granted, but he was the only shopkeeper who did this. He also kept tiny glasses into which he poured the pop of your choice and charged one penny. We'd ask each other: "Are you coming to Cook's Corner for a penny drink?"

Further down Edgeware Road on the opposite side stood Lamb's Dairy and we loved watching the huge metal urns being taken in and out. The lady who ran the shop had a huge bell at the top of the door which sounded as we went inside. The tiles on the floor were very ornate and a huge open space to walk across before you got to the highly polished solid wood counter. She spoke politely, and always greeted us with: "Goooooood Morrrrrrrrrning" or "Goooooooood Aaaaaaafternoon."

Hannah Street shared the backlane with Edgeware Road; my pal Katie Quinn lived there and her yard had a huge cellar. Further down the lane lived Gracie Robinson, her husband and three sons John, Albert and Peter. I loved going to their house when John's auntie visited. She knew sign language and she used to teach us something new every time she came.

Greenhow Place was the next along with a food store in the middle and a cobblers on the corner.

Trevor Atkinson was pals with Eric Hutchinson who lived at 3 Eveline Gardens. They used to go climbing in the derelict houses when they were around twelve years old. There was a much younger lad named Colin Alexander who was around nine years old. Trevor tells the story: "He was a fearless kid and he climbed up onto the roof of an old boozer, The Skiff, a rambling old pub. We heard a clatter, and the chimney stack which Colin was holding onto, collapsed and took him with it. Eric went as white as a sheet and we thought he'd been killed. He was lying in the back yard by the time we got down to where he was. The chimney had missed him by inches and, luckily, it hadn't landed on top of him. He was badly injured, but got back to full strength. It didn't stop him from climbing in the old houses."

Most of the time we stuck to our own few streets, but there were definite boundary lines. Ours began at Atkinson Road and ended between Edgeware Road and Gluehouse Lane, and if we strayed into a "foreign" camp there was big trouble. On sight of the enemy, names would be called first. Starting with phrases such as "My dad's bigger than your dad!" then degenerating to "You stink," and suchlike. Then the missiles would come raining down. We called it "Pelting stones."

Clara Street back lane looking down towards the Tyne. The top of St Columba's can be seen and what was left of the allotments. The photo was taken in 1968.

Buddle Road during demolition. The remains of Reggie Moore's shop can be seen at the corner of Maria Street and the steps leading down from the side door near the cellar.

Bob Speight remembers playing cricket in the back lane: "My Aunt Lizzie Hall lived at No 7 and her back yard faced the lane; it was a good place for a cricket pitch. Her windows were never in danger as her wall was where the stumps were drawn, but the Bramble's family were always replacing theirs. Bond Street in 1949 had washing houses in them and we used to go in there with nitrate film. Lots of it had been thrown out because it was banned and we found it outside an old film distribution place, they were old Charlie Chaplin movies. We took two feet of film and wrapped it into a tight cylinder then wrapped paper around it. Next we folded one side of the paper and twisted the other side to light. When the flames took hold, we stamped on it and it gave off an evil smell, probably the first stink bombs."

Belle Cross was a member of the Jolly Girls group at the Cochrane Street Club: "It started off as a private members' club in a couple of houses, a kind of business men's club. It closed down and moved to the new building when they built the shopping centre. It was then named the Key Club, the male members used a key to get in. I used to live at 69 Buddle Road on the gable end of Maughan Street."

In 1962 everyone got together in their own streets to prepare for the centenary of the Blaydon Races. Tables and chairs were brought out, with table cloths, decorations, streamers and party hats. Trevor Atkinson knows exactly where he was on the day: "When the Blaydon Races 1962 procession went by I was on the top of the old toilet block with my mates at the bottom of Scotswood Road – it was near Jobling Pursers at the bottom of Atkinson Road. We had a great view and saw all of the floats going by past all of the pubs. There was a W & H.O Wills one shaped like a giant cigarette with a filter tip, and a couple of penny farthing bikes and the City Council Pipe Band. Brian, a mate of my dad's, was playing the bass drum. I later became a drayman for the Scottish and Newcastle Breweries and I delivered the beer to the Crooked Billet and the Hydraulic Crane."

The Scottish and Newcastle Breweries float on Scotswood Road during the Centenary celebrations for the Blaydon Races in 1962.

About the same time, Buddle Road was being dug up to replace the old pipes. The work went on for months and the whole of the road was like the trenches. The women complained: "I'm sick of people trailing clarts through the house." But as kids it was a very interesting time, there were lots of Irish workmen on task who were full of chat and good humour and the surrounding mud heaps gave us hiding places when we acted out our favourite cowboy films. We'd be out there wearing our guns and holsters, it was literally the Wild West.

Maughan Street party to mark the Blaydon Races 1962 Centenary. Billy Danskin is leaning on a push chair and Irene Jacques walking towards the crowd. Margaret Welch is seated wearing a dark coat 3rd from the left. Mrs Rowntree far right at the front.

The Concrete Train on Buddle Road. It was built on the old Slidy area. Hugh Street and Clara Street back lanes can be seen in the background with Clabbies Shop to the left. Peter Moore (donator of this photo) can be seen wearing his trendy winkle picker shoes looking down from the large wheel. Sandra Bryson and Linda Liddle are talking together below and Yvonne Luscombe looking up wearing a dark coat. Others who have been identified to date are Randi Avilez, Katie Quinn, David Young and Dennis Larkham.

We all realised that things were changing around us. All of a sudden, it seemed that many of our pals and neighbours were speaking of new housing, booking furniture vans, changing schools etc. One friend of mine went to live in The Poplars, one of a set of high rise flats along Scotswood Road. The main entrance was decorated in a kind of pop art abstract pattern, but it only masked the problems faced by residents. Mothers with small children were isolated and couldn't allow their young children out to play alone because they couldn't supervise them. Old people missed the closeness of neighbours in the back to back streets. The lifts were always breaking down and the rubbish chutes stank all the year round, but more so in the summer.

Others were moving on, leaving buildings empty and a prime target for vandalism. We moved to 191 Hampstead Road and I made a new set of friends. We went to the West End Boys Club where there were many activities, art groups, sport, crafts etc. My pals were Dot Race and Kathleen Nevin. Our favourite music at the time was Tamla Motown, we knew all of the words and sang together on our way back from the club. Kath Welch went away to university and we lost touch for a while. She came back when David and I were married in 1973, but then she met her husband to be and they toured around India and other places. Just over a year ago, I was at an old school reunion and someone had Kath's telephone number. She was living in Woodbridge in Suffolk. She came up here to Newcastle to visit and since then has stayed with us a few times as well as visiting her mam Margaret who now lives in Consett.

We have also kept in touch with Peter Moore and his brother Johnny. Their dad Reggie was a colourful character who ran the corner shop with his wife Elsie on the junction of Buddle Road and Maria Street. There are regular reunions, usually held at the West Denton Fire Station Social Club in October or November and it's great to see old faces and talk about the good old days. We also go to the Fairholm Club to see old friend Nancy. It was her 60th birthday party and a huge spread was laid on. Sixty – where has all of the time gone?

Carol Young and Sheila Varley stand behind David Young in Frank Street. The Baptist Church building can be seen in the back ground.

Stephen Armstrong sitting in his pram at the top of Edgeware Road. Buddle Road back lane can be seen to the left and beyond that is the No 1 bus stop. To the right just around the bend was Mr Cook's shop leading around to St John's Road.

Easter Sunday in Maughan Street. Back row: Kathleen Welch, Lorraine Mountain, Linda Mountain, (Mrs Wilson's legs). Front row: Stephen Malone, Irene Jacques, Billy Danskin, and Stephen Mountain.

Edna Phipps enjoying a toffee apple outside a house in Maughan Street. Edna's brothers were Harry and Robert.

A house party in Violet Street.

Sparky, Lilian Barclay's dog. The photo was taken in the back yard of their home in Clara Street. Sparky is in front of the outside toilet door.

Irene Jacques with cousins David and Gloria Kirk.

Shirley Nicholson and Sylvia Kirk sitting on the wall in Maughan Street.

Agnes Jacques, Daisy Tennant, Phylis Fish and Mrs Wilson. The women are sitting on a wall in Maughan Street wearing their aprons and slippers. Could they have bought goods from a street merchant? They have towels and boxes and Daisy has her purse ready on her lap.

The Peddie sisters. Left to right: Margaret Alice, Nellie, Adeline and Lydia. Unfortunately, the name of the sister on the right is unknown. Can any reader identify her?

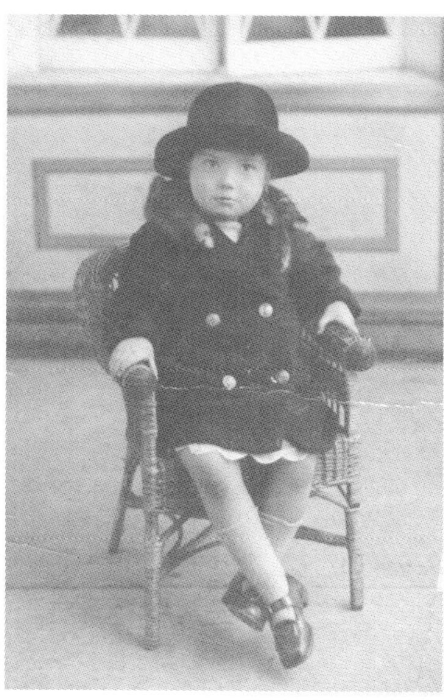

Mary Parks aged three years old wearing a fetching double breasted coat with fur collar and bowler hat, around 1927/8.

A group of friends about to play football. David Young is holding the ball. John Taylor is in the dark top, standing right. Eric Williams is crouching in the middle.

A Great Community
by Jimmy & Irene Barclay

Jimmy Barclay was born in 1937 at 79 Hugh Street, Benwell. He was one of nine children born to Margaret (Coulson) and Billy Barclay. The others were Billy, Peggy, Ronnie, Betty, Connie, Mary, Eric and Judy. He was evacuated during the war along with his elder sister Peggy to Langwathby in Penrith, but he was only two at the time. He married Irene who lived in the Elswick area.

"We had no telly when we were kids. We had to take the wireless battery to a shop on Scotswood Road to be charged, it was called an accumulator."

Jimmy and Irene Barclay in their home on Chapel House looking through old photos.

He remembers: "Hugh Street backed onto Frank Street and we shared a back lane with Clara Street. Down the back of Clara Street back lane at the top of School Street, there was the Mission, St Columba's. We went to Sunday School there and you got a lovely brightly coloured stamp to stick in your book. It encouraged us to go.

"At the top of Hugh Street lived Eva Nicholson, her dad was a builder who did the local repairs. He worked in the cellar of his house and we could see him in there from the street; we'd sit down and watch him. There was also a shop at the top of Adelaide Terrace and Clara Street and it stunk of fire lighters. McLean's was on the corner and George's the butchers was next door, then after the back lane there was Clabbies between Hugh Street lane. They sold sweets, chocolate and groceries. There was also a fruit cart that came around the doors – Mr Stevenson who used to come for his dinner and leave the horse in the street. When he put the nose bag on it and went inside we used to fill ourselves with fruit before he came back."

"If any of the mothers sent us for a message we got a slice of bread." Jimmy's wife, Irene, recalls: "It was considered a real treat back then. Another real treat was when we could go to Eckhards Muffin Factory on Scotswood Road to buy a muffin for a halfpenny. There was a pub or a shop on every corner. There used to be a fish shop called The Toll Bar, it was opposite the Hydraulic Crane pub. We'd get a paper of chips and eat them outside."

Jimmy loved going to the pictures: "I never had enough money to go to see a film, so I'd go around the doors asking if I could take the bottles back to the shop for a bit of cash, but I still didn't have enough, so I'd take myself off around to my elder sister Peggy's house in Aline Street to ask her. She'd say 'No, go away, I haven't got any money' so I'd lock myself in to her outside toilet, we called it a lavvy back then. I could cry and scream for ages, then she would come out and say 'Here's threepence.' Then I would say 'Shove it under the door' and stop crying then unlock the door and run as fast as I could to the cinema. We went to the Crown, Majestic, the Rex and sometimes to the Odeon in town. We loved the cowboy films, our favourites starred Roy Rogers or Gary Cooper. In the good end it cost 6d but in the dog end (as we called it) it was only 4d. When we came out we would slap our thighs as we pretended to be the cowboys. Not often, but sometimes we went to the 'Loppy Opera' on Condercum Road. We also enjoyed watching *The Three Stooges* – Curly, Larry and Moe."

"We were never in the house in the school holidays. We loved going up to Wylam for the day and we always came back famished and the mothers would say 'Here's the kids back' then they would go inside to cook something for tea. My mam always baked stottie cakes.

"Liquorice root was a favourite of mine and Locust Dry. I'd chew it until it went

The interior of the Majestic when it became a cinema in 1954. The usherette is wearing a paisley wrap over style pinney. The children are all packed together; if the film was popular and too many children turned up, they would be asked to share a seat.

soggy, put it in my pocket when it went hard and then take it out the next day and chew it again. Sometimes we went to the fish shop along the Pipe Track Lane – Oliver's. Someone would buy a loaf of bread to share out and if you had a bottle of pop you'd share it with your pals and there would be lots of crumbs floating around in there but we didn't mind."

Irene used to like to eat Tripe: "It was raw and I couldn't eat it now" but Jimmy liked Boily when he was a kid. It was made with hot water and milk till it all went sloppy. "He still likes his porridge like that and he just drinks it out of the cup. We didn't get any sweets, just food like mince and dumplings."

"When the gas man came, he would empty the meter. We all stood around the table to watch as he stacked up all the pennies in towers. When he was finished he always gave mam some back, it was a divi, a kind of a bonus."

"I got blamed for everything that happened in the street." Irene laughed: "90% of the time it was you."

"I didn't half get some chases from people," he remembers. "If a football went into someone's yard, nine times out of ten the wifey wouldn't give it back. So, we used to catch a cat and put it in her outside toilet, then catch another, then another. When all three cats were locked in and by the time the woman came to open the door they were as high as kites and would scramble hissing and scratching out of there. We'd go off and say 'That'll fettle her.'

The Pipe Track Lane. This photo was taken in 1971.

"We played Tally Ho in the streets. There were two teams. One team ran away and the other team would capture them and take them to the bay. Somebody would be picked to guard the bay then they would escape and we'd catch them and we'd swap over teams. We could play that all day.

"Another thing we did was to tie a rope around the old door knobs on a couple of front doors, then knock and when the householder tried to get out, they couldn't. We were young and we didn't ever think about if there had been a fire in the house how they would get out."

"Scraper was popular – the game was played for money and we used to gamble. Everyone stood about six to ten yards away from the path and money was thrown to land in the gulley along the path from the gutter. If we could get hold of an old bicycle wheel, we took the spokes out and the tyre off and would run for miles booling it along with a stick.

"I remember at school when Mr Clarke was the headmaster. We were playing football in the yard and one of the lads fell over. I got the blame and the big lads took me to the teacher. He belted me twelve times on each hand and I was screaming. I ran home and my mam was hopping mad when she saw the bruises on my arms. She stormed up to the school and hit the teacher. He was shouting 'Get the caretaker, get the caretaker.' He would have been suspended now for inflicting those marks. Mr Tweddle used to have this old heavy push bike and at 4 o'clock, when school finished every night, we all used to beat a hasty retreat out of the door. He always collared one of the lads to push his bike up Atkinson Road and onto Armstrong Road.

"When I was around eight years old, me and a pal, Ellison Cleminson, used to make burners. We would use an old tin, poke holes through the bottom with a nail, then make a handle from a piece of wire. The tin was used to light a fire in from bits of wood and paper to get a bleezer. One day, it was so windy that we put it inside an air vent where a brick was loose at the side of the welfare building at the top of Clara Street. We couldn't believe it when we saw the whole flu go up, the building was well alight. We ran away and the fire brigade was called, but it was too late. A policeman came to our house, but I was hiding behind the cupboard, I'd been there all day. My mam didn't know where I was, I was too scared to come out. The next day, when the fire had died down, we all went in and came out with bottles of orange juice and tins of burnt National Milk and Oster milk. We were smacking our lips with the toffee tasting powder.

"When I was about ten years old, my dad was run over by a tram car. It was 65 years ago. He was hospitalised for a long time but he pulled through. The trolley buses were all over the place then. If one got stuck the bus driver behind had to get a huge pole to take the broken down bus from the track so that he could go ahead.

"Sometimes we would go to Hodgkin Park – it was lovely. There was the top end which had a tennis court. The bottom part had a bowling green, drinking fountain, band stand and another lovely bowling green. The parky used to walk around with his stick and the kids wouldn't have dared to step on the grass, he would have hit them. If you did stand on it and, the parky reported you to your mother, you would get a hiding.

"Me and my pals used to just about live in the Bond Street baths. We didn't have swimming costumes. Our mams would use an old woollen jumper, the kind with the buttons on the side of the neck. It would be cut in a scoop neck style and the arms cut out. It was tied around the middle with a snake belt and we all had one of those. But, when we jumped in the water it fell off and the soggy

Hodgkin Park Bowling Green as it was in 1920.

woollen suit would be down to your ankles as it stretched. They weighed a ton when wet.

"On wash day my mam hung the clothes on a line across the lane. When she was finished she picked us kids up one by one and we were bathed in the same water. As the linen hung on the line, if the ash man came or we rode our bikes through the sheets there'd be trouble. The ash was kept in those tin bins with a lid on. In the winter, we used to use the ash to trail along the bottom of the streets so that out sledges didn't go onto the Scotswood Road. Our Billy made me a great sledge when he worked at Vickers, it had metal irons on the bottom.

"There was lino on the floor, we called it Tarry Toot, and there was always a proggy or a clippy mat on top. We used to help to make the mats. The pieces had to be cut in two inch lengths by about three quarters of an inch. There were two wooden slats with canvas rolled around and you'd work with it in front of you progging from one side to the other. When it was done it was trimmed to make it even. Usually they were on the bed for twelve months, then used on the floor, by then a new one had been made for the bed.

"I left South Benwell School in 1952 and my first job was as an electrician's apprentice, second as a coachbuilder, then to Mitchell Bearings as a moulder. But, I didn't settle at any of those jobs and, even though they were all apprenticeships. I started at Churchill Redman and served my time as a toolmaker there until I was 21."

"Jobs were easy to get, you could literally walk into a new job off the streets," said Irene.

"When I was 16, the blokes from work used to watch me run up the road, to get the tram car from Clara Street along Armstrong Road to see Irene when we were courting. The men used to pile onto the tram cars till you couldn't move, then more of them used to hang onto the back cage. You could hear the sound of boots running up the streets, especially up Water Street.

"When we got married, we were offered a flat above Jones' wet fish shop at the bottom of Clara Street. Mrs Walker had the key. We went to see it, and I said 'I'm not living here, it's filthy!' But the whole family rallied around and got it cleaned up and decorated, it was lovely. When we had our first baby, the steps were too high to get the pram into the house, so we had to take the steps out to push it into the hallway. We didn't get any advice on buying our own place back then and it's something we regretted, although we have our own property now. People just didn't even know that it was possible to be a home owner then."

Irene said: "We were in the prime position to watch the 1962 Centenary of the Blaydon Races. Our flat had windows which all looked out onto the Scotswood Road where the processions all went past. The whole family came down to ours and we were all just about hanging out of the windows to see. We had a bird's eye view."

"I can still remember my mother's check number for the dividend at the shops," says Irene. "Mam's was 145679 and my grannie's was 695108, but don't ask me what I did yesterday," she jokes. "People got on well, they stuck together and they are still friends now – a great community."

Middlemass Float advertising their biscuits. Notice in the background the cigarettes hoarding advertising Gold Leaf.

The Guinness float goes by during the 1962 Blaydon Races Centenary.

Still Kickin'
by Lilian Barclay

Lilian was born at 82 Frank Street in 1943, a cousin to Jimmy Barclay and her parents were Alec and Rene Barclay. She is also second cousin to my husband David Young and remembers David's mother well: "Whenever we went to Mary Young's house she always offered us a cup of tea. We used to laugh how Mary would leave the gas oven alight to save money on matches!"

Lilian went messages for her and she recalled the shops in the area; at the bottom of Clara Street. Tommy Lee had a fruit shop, Lilian went in one day and pinched a plum.

"Kay Simpson's mam saw me but she didn't tell my mam. I went into the outside toilet to eat it, but afterwards I was sick with worry. There was also a fish shop to the left of the street that sold crabs' legs. The post office was next to Tommy's and it also sold wool. I used to go to Bob's the butchers. I'd look for his dustpan and brush to sweep up all of the sawdust and end up with a huge pile of it in one corner. When I left the shop he used to scatter it all around again. Granny Larkham lived at the bottom of the street in an old shop which had been a general dealers."

Rene Barclay (Lilian's mother) and pals raising a glass of beer at the Old Hall Social Club. Rene is far left of the photo.

Lilian's mother worked as a seamstress for a company on Scotswood Road and always swore by the quality of Marks and Spencers clothing, which was manufactured there. Her mother Rene used to say that there were dozens of supervisors there and that only so many stitches were allowed in each inch, otherwise the garment would be rejected. Rene also made all of their clothing at home.

Tommy Barclay, Lilian's brother, was in the RNVR aboard the *Calliope*. When he was on leave she could earn 3d to blanco his hat. He owned a motorbike which she polished for a small fee. Tommy had no sense of direction and often got lost when the bike broke down and couldn't find his way back. She also had a Saturday job at Woolworths on Clayton Street when she was 13 years old. She received five shillings for the day, the equivalent today would be around 25p. She recalls that she worked hard for the money.

"My mam said that as I was earning so much cash she could stop my pocket money, so I was no better off. There was a jewellery shop on Adelaide Terrace, I think it was Clarke's, and I saved up by putting 3d or 6d a week and bought a rhinestone necklace for my mam for Christmas – she still has it now. I also spent money at the cinema and I queued to see John Wayne starring in *The Quiet Man*. One day I only had a halfpenny, so I took a glass jam jar as part payment. The glass was recycled as it was in short supply. Me and my pals paid to go in the cheap end, then we would pretend to go to the toilet and change seats.

Tommy Barclay sporting his Teddy Boy quiff.

Lilian and her family also lived in an upstairs flat in 17 Clara Street from when she was about two years old to fifteen. She remembers some of the neighbours who lived nearby. Meggie Cheetham lived next door, she had the downstairs flat and Michael Gillender was in the next one up. Her grandad, Thomas Maxwell, was a champion swimmer. He was also an excellent pianist who played in most of the pubs along Scotswood Road. Granny Maxwell, as she was known as, caused much hilarity one day. She sent Lilian's uncle Alan to the shops for a saveloy but didn't know the correct spelling so she drew a picture of it.

Her dad was an electric welder for Barfords on Scotswood Road. He was offered a job in the Grantham area and it meant that Lilian, at the age of fifteen, would have to make new friends. It took her a while to settle in the new place. As she was still working for Woolworths, the company arranged for her to transfer to a local branch. Another family shared the house at Arnoldfield, which Lilian recalls as having a huge driveway. Her bedroom was in what used to be the library which had wooden covered walls and huge glass doors.

"My bed was in the middle of the room on a carpet, and nothing else in there except a music box covered in shells. One night when I was in bed, I could hear scratching. I was terrified, facing the wall and I didn't dare move, then the music box began to play. I stayed in that position until morning, Later in the day I was talking to the gardener and he told me that when it was a family home, a male member of staff murdered a female colleague, then buried her. The body was discovered some time later under the window of the library. He threw himself onto a railway line.

Shirley Nicholson and Lilian Barclay. Notice the bouffant hairstyles.

"Just when I had made friends and started to feel more settled, my mam wasn't happy there, she missed our relatives and friends – so, one year later, we returned to Newcastle. The first night back we had to stay at the Denton Hotel until we got a house at Denton Square. It was difficult to start up friendships again. I got a job at the Co-op in the fuel department."

Hair styles were popular with Lilian and her friends and they would sit for ages "Doing their hair". She laughs: "The bigger the hair the better! Margaret, a good pal of mine, couldn't get her hair high enough, so she used to roll up old nylons and stuff them among the tatting. We used to wear garters before suspender belts were fashionable, and one day I felt something flapping around my ankle. When I looked down the stocking had fallen, so I just stepped out of it." She also remembered some of her friends wore skirts with wire hoops in the hems and when they got onto the bus to sit down the whole lot went up like a lamp shade. "There was always a crowd of lads hanging around the bottom of the escalators in Fenwicks – a poor fashion design!"

Lilian met Keith Allinson and he later became a member of a band named The Teambeats. The group toured the Co-op halls and church halls and she remembers that only teas, coffees and soft drinks were sold. Keith was two years younger than his brother Peter who played with Hank Marvin and Bruce Welch before they went away to London and became The Shadows. They used to practice in the loft at the Allinson home in Wingrove Road. It was such a huge house and there was a snooker table in the attic.

She married Keith Allinson in 1965 and the Beatles were a popular band then. She remembers Keith singing 'She Loves You'. Among many names, the band became Alive and Kickin' which toured the local social clubs. Lilian said that they would all go in by the back door of a club and she helped to carry in the equipment with her friends. Back then, the committee men's wives sat in reserved seats, and other club members were afraid to sit there, but Lilian always paid, even though she could have got in free, then she could sit where she liked. On one occasion the band played at a place in Gretna. The cinema, dance and wrestling ring were all in the same building, so if anyone misbehaved and were barred they spoiled themselves for any of the activities. The manager showed them around and they were treated like royalty with dressing room, sandwiches laid on and teas and coffees. A stark contrast to the set up in the northern clubs, where often Lilian and her pals were directed away from seats with the phrase "You can't sit there, they belong to someone who always sits there." Some years later the band was renamed Still Kickin'.

Old Friends
by Bob Speight

"A certain Austrian gentleman had declared war and Newcastle City Council fearing possible gas attacks sent all expectant mums to Gilsland Hospital in 1939. My mother, Isabelle, was one and was joined by Mrs Margaret Wilson, Mrs Baldwin, who lived in the council flats on Condercum Road, and Mrs Yare. I was born on 2nd October 1939 and officially a Cumbrian. There were four lads all born together – me, Kenny Bramble, Matty Baldwin and Robin Wilkinson. It was decided that there wasn't going to be an attack and I was brought back to No 9 Ash Street. Our family took it over from a family named Collingwood. Henry Percival Collingwood's son Harry married my mother's sister Margaret Poppleton. Another sister of my mother's was Elizabeth Hall (née Poppleton) she lived at No 7. Her husband Sidney worked at Vickers Armstrong's in the tank shop, he was also an excellent swimmer and swam across the Tyne.

"Ash Street was a typical downstairs flat with a glass door into the front bedroom and a cupboard under the stairs. Me and my pal Kenny Bramble used to lift the floor boards up and get under the house, all of the wires were hanging down dangerously, but it was an adventure to us. The living room had a cast iron range with a hot water boiler on one side, there was a fireplace in every room. Three stairs led into the kitchen where a cast iron bowl three feet in diameter was, under that we could put a fire. Coal was fed through a little hole about three feet square from the back lane. The shops sold candles, there was hardly any light and we cooked on the fire when we had coal."

Kenny Bramble (left) and Bob Speight. The photo was taken in Bond Street around 1950/51.

Bob's first school was Canning Street where he went from 1945-6. He remembers: "The winters were abominable, no coal or coke, no electricity, there were gas shortages. The snow was so deep, there used to be layers upon layers of snow – snow shower after snow shower. In between a new fall of clean white snow, there'd be layers of soot, it looked just like a giant sandwich."

A clear memory for Bob is the colour of the bread: "The Americans had stopped shipping wheat and the British home grown variety was a grey colour on the outside crust, then another layer – it didn't taste like bread."

Canning Street School. The school was opened in 1903 and closed December 1990. The new school on this site was opened in January 1991.

"I went to Atkinson Road School from 1951-1955, it was a workshop and engineering school and only lads attended then. We made callipers, did surface gauging, flat and straight plates. I became an engineer, Robert Speight AMI Mech E. Others that went there were Geoffrey Cook, a Newcastle City Councillor, Bill Scott of *Wotcher Geordie* fame and Neville Walton who whose family lived in Gill Street."

This photo shows the industrial machines at Atkinson Road Technical School where Bob learned his skills. Bob said: "It was known as Akky Tech Metal Work Shop. There was a brazing hearth and anvil in a recess to the right hand side of the door."

During the 1953 Coronation, Bob took part in making a huge Union Jack from coloured paper strips. They marked the lengths out first on the floor and everyone strung them across the whole area of the balcony criss crossing over. Bob Scoley was the teacher and most of his class were there.

"There's a photo somewhere of that event, it was taken by Mr Wright, the maths teacher. He was an ex-prisoner of war in the Royal Northumberland Fusiliers. They used to call him Tiger Wright, one of the first captured before Dunkirk and spent all of the war in prison. He used to tell us stories of how when their razor blades were useless and him and his pals would put them into the pigswill for the German pigs to eat. He used to shout: 'Smith ... Is this your maths book?' when he found a mistake but his bark was worse than his bite."

To celebrate the Coronation in 1953 the pupils created a Union Jack which stretched across the veranda of the upper floor of the school. Mr R. (Dickie) Dowell can be seen to the far left of the photo. Bob's form master was Mr R. (Bob) Scholey. Pupils: Bob Speight, Brian Walker, Ian Scott Forbes, ? Milburn, ? McGowan, John Bensley, Anthony Evans, John Watt, Daniel Webb, unknown, possibly Brian Bessford. The photo was taken by Mr Wright (Tiger Wright).

The hall which was used as a dining room and gym, the bars can be seen behind the pupils. From left to right back row: John Watt, ? Radley, Daniel Webb, unknown, McGowan, Anthony Evans, Alan Robson, Chris Randall, Frank ? Middle row: Colin Tortoise, unknown, John Bensley, ? Milburn, Raymond Yare, Michael Froggat, ? Minneken, Brian Curry. Front row: unknown, Robert Speight, Phil Jobling, unknown, Peter Dalkin, Alan Roberts, Phil Beckingham, Ian Scott Forbes, Brian Bessford. Form Master at right is Mr R. (Bob) Scholey. The photo was taken by Mr Wright.

Bob was never any good at exams, but he remained in the A class, and after four years he could stay on for an extra 12 months.

"I still remained paly with Robin Wilkinson, he lived in the manager's cottage on the old pit site on Condercum Road. We used to play in the grounds. There were 80ft by 80ft reservoirs, six to seven feet deep and there was a pit in one of them where a draining valve was. We loved that one, it had toads and newts in there.

"Isabella Colliery was owned by Newcastle City Council and used as an engineering depot, the other two thirds of it was used by Ross' Pickles. The old building is still standing but roofless. The pit shafts were still there, but railed off, and we used to hop over the wall and drop twelve feet down to throw stones into the pits."

When Bob lived in Ash Street he recalled being in bed and hearing a man walking up the street very early tapping against the wall with a steel tipped ferule.

"It was the deputy walking up to the pit at Slatyford Road at about four o'clock in the morning, a hell of a walk before a full day's shift."

Bob's dad used to love reading westerns, there was a one penny book shop on Clara Street where he bought novels. "My old man read all of Zane Grey's writing – *The Thundered Herd* and *Riders of the Purple Sage*. He also liked a flutter on the horses and he'd put 2/- each way on Ned Kelly. He never signed his name and used a pen name because betting was illegal. I took his bet around to the bookies who was situated in the back lane of Larch Street and Ash Street. The back door would open and you'd go down to the washing shed window, the door was locked. Then I'd say 'Can I place this bet?' My dad told me 'If you see a policeman, don't go in!' One day, as I was half way down the lane I saw a policeman and the bookie walking away."

When his dad became crippled with arthritis he remembers that his mam returned to work at a bakery, a family run company – she specialised in cakes. She was also on a stand at the Great Co-op Exhibition and got a commemorative watch and a shoe horn stamped with Great Exhibition.

"There were lots of little shops around – Storey's at the top of Clara Street and the junction of Adelaide Terrace. There was a barber who lived at Westfield Gardens, his shop had a wooden floor covered in sawdust. He sold just about everything in there, bicycle tyres, nuts, bolts, hinges ... and the first thing you smelled when you walked in was mothballs, he sold hundreds of firelighters. He sold watch and clincher shells operated by batteries, then he would charge them up for folks. One thing I remember was that girls were not allowed in the barbers because they sold contraceptives and they weren't supposed to see them. When a man had his hair cut, the barber would brush the hair away from the back of his neck and ask 'Would Sir like anything for the

A sports day held at the Benwell Cricket Club grounds. Bob Speight's photo shows the pupils dressed smartly for the event. The lad at the back of the photo wearing glasses and looking down is was called Best and the lad with folded arms at the far bottom right hand corner is Richard Tong.

weekend?' We didn't know what he meant when the man would hand over 2/6d and we never saw what he bought. At the corner of Ash Street and Adelaide Terrace, Duncan's the grocers sold broken biscuits. On the other corner was Maypole the grocers, the woman who ran that shop was lucky she wasn't poisoned. When she reached from her bed to a cup on a table for a drink, it had Domestos in there."

He recalls that at the bottom of Ash Street looking down towards Clara Street on the right hand corner was the opticians, then Ritchie's the fruiterers and nearby, Duncan's the grocers. There was also an off license which gave one penny back on a returned bottle. "Lawson's fish shop was in the back lane between Bond Street and Ash Street. Bramble's shoe repair shop was just up from there. Cockburn's fruit and veg shop and a butcher's shop which was run by George Mead; it was small with a single counter and sawdust on the floor. He was a canny fella, very chatty. They used to take half carcases in there to put in the fridge – half a cow or half a pig."

Bob described the Benwell Hotel pub on Adelaide Terrace: "It was a very old pub, and on Good Friday the Benwell Harriers race started from there. The prominent people of the day stood on the balcony to look down on the race. When you went into the main door you were confronted by a huge set of stairs, then the right hand door went into the main saloon. By the 1940s it was still frowned on for a single woman to go into a pub, so they'd go into what was known as the Jug End where they could go to have a jug of ale filled up, sometimes they could have a quiet half in there."

He pondered the exact location of the dentists surgery: "I think that Beck's the dentists was near Hugh Gardens on Adelaide Terrace, maybe above the Boots shop. My old man would sooner tie a piece of string to his tooth and slam the door. I don't think it was the pulling of the teeth or the anaesthetic, but on the wall there was a huge cabinet and in it he had collected examples of teeth he'd pulled. They were the most horrible teeth that I had ever seen. Going to the doctor ... ours was Dr Desilvera, he was Portuguese and had married an English woman – he was a real nice guy. Their surgery was in the front room of a house at a time when they made all of their own pills with all of his own equipment. They canvassed for patients just before the NHS came into force in 1947. His son was a doctor and he also bred Staffordshire Bull Terriers."

“Dees, on Adelaide Terrace, was a clothing and habedashery. They used overhead cash canisters and they would take your money from you, put it in a wooden cylinder, screw it into the overhead contraption overhead, pull a handle and it would spring and rush along to the office. All cash was sorted out away from the counter, the office staff would look at the bill, put in the change and zing, it went back to the counter before the assistant had finished wrapping the goods.”

Two members of staff at one of the branches of Boots in the West End.

Bob said that fashions were governed by the war. At that time his mother worked in a baker’s shop on Conhope Lane: “The sacks which held a hundred weight of flour were made of very good quality cotton and my mother kept them and made them into sheets and pillowcases. She even made dresses in 1946 and I remember going with mam, Aunt Lizzie and Aunt Winnie to town to spend the coupons on dresses. In 1946 there were no shoes available, only clogs which only lasted about a year. Coupons were removed in 1948 and restrictions were lifted. There used to be a funny little symbol which resembled two closed Cs on clothing, a kind of utility mark. Until 1948 everything that was made was in restricted amounts, dresses, shirts all had to conform, then we saw the beginning of economic recovery.”

He remembered kids fashions like leather pilot’s helmets – “Which kept your lugs warm.” Silk scarves were still in fashion in the late 1940s and early ’50s and people wore trilbys and peaked caps. “From 1948 we saw the new look, flared skirts, dresses, blouses and hats with veils on the top to keep them on. The veil was never over the face, but gauzy like hair.”

One of the many Co-ops buildings in the area which had similar fixtures and fittings as Bob describes. A Jimmy Forsyth photo dated 1956.

The Co-op was a huge building and Bob described the inside as having a U shaped counter by the side of the door with huge cupboards and drawers. There was a billiard hall upstairs, but they were warned off going near there – it was considered a den of iniquity. Bob remembers that it took up the whole block. Butter was not available, but they could obtain margarine and he liked the Kosher butter: "We weren't Jewish, but we ate it and it tasted better than the standard stuff which tasted of axle grease."

Bob enjoyed visits to the cinema: "The Grand (the loppy opera) was a fabulous place. The massive double doors opened on the Elswick Road side. The ABC minors showed cartoons at 10 o'clock in the morning and we could watch two for 1/- and one B feature movie. We particularly enjoyed a film called *The Whistler*. It was a mystery, on for 40 minutes. It started with a shadow of a man, then an odd whistling tune. We liked Gene Autry films and *Blythe Spirit* by Noel Coward."

Bob says that Robin Wilkinson's sister, Margaret, who was four years younger than Robin, was mad on Ballet. "Her folks paid for her tuition and she was accepted by the Ballet Rambert, her stage name was Maggy Tait." (Janet, Bob's wife, saw her there when she went to visit their daughter Fleur.) "At the time the company was in a state of flux as it had always been known for a particular style of ballet. I was best man at Robin's wedding, he moved to Milton Keynes and was working as a civil engineer."

"Other pals I remember were Keith Crombie, who runs a jazz club now in Pink Lane. He was a talent spotter for View Carre Jazz Club in Gibson Street, Byker and from there he ended up running the club in Pink Lane. Kenny Bramble moved to Canada when he was about 28. When the trolley buses came onto Adelaide terrace Robin Wilkinson's dad was part of a team who ripped up the old tram lines. One lad who worked for him was the youngest steam roller driver ever."

Bob is still married to Janet and they are both active in their support of the Friends of Tyne Riverside Country Park at Newburn. Five years ago they held a commemoration of the Battle of Newburn. Janet prepared a video and disc of the event which is on sale at the centre for £5 each. Last year some of the filming was done by Janet at the exhibition Comitatus which was a demonstration of the Roman Army of tactics and weapons. The group received at £23,000 grant from English Heritage for the Battle of Newburn event and around 5,000 people attended. For Comitatus, they received £600 from the Newburn Council and 1,000 people enjoyed the day's events. Bob proudly says of Janet: "She is a true cockney, born within the sounds of the four bells."

Bob and Margaret Wilkinson in Condercum Road pit yard.

Right: Bob reading the book 'All the Lads and Lasses' at his home.

The Corner Shop
by Linda Sutton (née Scott)

Linda Sutton (née Scott) was born in Benwell in the 1950s and has lived and taught in the area all her life. Her father Billy was the youngest son of Frank and Hannah Scott. Frank and his eldest son Adam worked in the 'Charley' (Charlotte) Pit on Condercum Road. In 1930 Adam was killed at the age of thirty, and in 1936 his father was also killed, near to where his son had died. He was fifty years old. Another son, Frank was injured in the Montagu Pit in 1935, and being unable to work as a miner he set up a shop. Billy avoided going down the mines; working for Walter Willsons in Haltwhistle, he met Olive Tweddell, whom he later married while on leave during World War Two.

Right: Linda's parents on their wedding day outside 73 Denton Gardens. They are the couple to the right. The bridesmaid was Linda's mum's sister Nellie and the best man, her mum's cousin-in-law Cecil Batey. Linda said: "Mum, who had 'joined up' was entitled to leave for her honeymoon. When it didn't come through on time, she went AWOL, leaving my grandma fearing the arrival of the military police."

Linda recalls a much loved family business:
"F & D Scott's, which stood at the corner of Colston Street and Wellfield Road, was the little business which became the focus of Scott family gatherings for many years to come. I was born in 1952, and have many very happy family memories which centre on 'the shop'.

"Every Sunday, after lunch, the clan would convene, and off we would set – Seaton Sluice if it was fine (and the sun usually shone in those days) or, if there was considered to be the threat of a 'sea fret' we'd head inland to places like Chollerford or Hexham. Those of the family without cars would be squeezed into the cars of those who had. Frank's pride and joy was his BSA car, christened Genevieve. His injuries having left him unable to drive, my father, Billy, would take the wheel. As the baby of the family (being the child of the youngest brother), I was always on someone's lap. Upon arrival at the chosen spot, camp would be set up, and the primus stove would soon be on the go, for the first all-important brew of tea. If the weather was cold, it didn't matter – being outside and together was what counted, and there were always plenty of tartan rugs to huddle beneath. At the end of the afternoon, the convoy would return to 'the shop' for tea – a proper spread, all home-made; I remember particularly Auntie Doris' (meat) mince pies. Then it was washing-up by committee, his pipe for Uncle Frank, cigarettes for most of the others, and more cups of tea. Sometimes there would be a game of 'Beetle', or Bingo.

"On fine days the door of the shop was permanently open, but on cooler days the jangle of the brass bell would summon Frank or Doris through from their sitting-room, he in his brown shop-coat, she in a checked overall. This was more than a place to buy groceries: people met their neighbours here, frequently staying to chat to both shopkeepers and other customers. News was exchanged, opinions expressed about everything from the weather to football. It was a place very much at the heart of the community it served. Few people had the luxury of a private phone in those days, so messages for neighbours were frequently taken and passed on. I don't recall my aunt and uncle ever experiencing any trouble, but I do remember that Uncle Frank kept a heavy lead cosh hanging behind the bedroom door.

"Just inside the door stood the bag of potatoes, with their scale and broad metal scoop-shaped pan. I learned at an early age how to use the correct combinations of hexagonal metal weights to measure out half and quarter stones. I must have been quite young when I was allowed to serve in the shop, but I was good at mental

An aerial view of the new Canning Street School which was built to replace the old structure. Linda says that the entrance to the new school is roughly where the Scott family shop stood.

arithmetic and wasn't shy – my position in the family meant that I was well used to adult company.

"The wooden counter had a wonderful inlaid brass yard measure in it, which I still have, although I cannot remember anything being sold which required measuring! The red and silver bacon-slicer, which cut bacon and ham to the required thickness with a rather malicious swishing sound, I was never allowed to touch, but the display of sweets in the window was another matter. This I was allowed to arrange to my satisfaction. Sherbet fountains and dips, foam 'sea creatures', aniseed balls, ABCs, packets of chewing-gum with cards to collect (*The Man from UNCLE* in the late 1960s), candy cigarettes, sweet tobacco, Black Jacks, Fruit Salads, Refreshers, Parma Violets ... Beneath this was where the sticks – a necessary item in those days of open coal fires – were kept; splintery bundles secured with twists of wire. I always imagined that there must be mice under there, although I never saw one.

"A glass display unit on the counter protected a small selection of fresh cakes, and on the top of this stood the jars of sweets; when I was old enough to reach, I was allowed to serve these. (Cherry Lips, multi-coloured sherbet, 'Italian' fudge, Clarnico mint creams, pineapple chunks, rhubarb and custards, sherbet lemons and those large cuboid caramels coated in pink or white icing.) Behind the assistant were shelves from which tinned goods, bags of sugar, tea, loose butter and cigarettes were served.

"A metal stand held large square tins of Tudor Crisps. The tins bore the image of Henry the Eighth, and each packet of plain crisps contained a blue paper twist of salt. Tins of loose biscuits were on the same fixture, the broken remnants of which were sold off cheaply.

"The till was a large wooden drawer – no mechanics involved – beautifully smooth from much use, allowing the change to slide out easily from the sloping compartments. My mother bought the bulk of our groceries from the shop, and in the 1950s these were still referred to as the weekly 'rations'.

"Frank and Doris died in the early 1970s; the shop is long-demolished. The Scott boys all went to Canning Street, and from 1983 until 2008 I was a teacher at the school, I remained there for twenty-five years. Initially at the original three-storey red-brick edifice, and then later the new open-plan rebuild. The second Canning Street has also undergone many changes, being extended and remodelled in 2008. The entrance to the new school is just where the shop actually stood, and as I arrived or left my place of work I would often think of my family and the important place in my childhood of F & D Scott's corner shop."

Now retired Linda enjoys working with the West Newcastle Picture History Collection group. She has recently been involved in the preparation of teaching notes to accompany sets of photos of bygone Benwell. With Lottery funding, these are being distributed to local primary schools.

A Scott family wedding. Frank Scott is shown at the far right. He was later to be killed in the Charlotte Pit. From left to right. Hannah, Billy, Tom, Alec, John and Frank.

MINER KILLED AND TWO HURT

Buried By Stone Fall In Benwell Pit

TRAGIC WIDOW

Son Victim of Previous Accident

ONE MAN was killed and two were injured by a fall of stone to-day in the Charlotte Pit of Elswick Coal Co., in Condercum Road, Benwell, Newcastle.

The dead man was

Frank Scott (59), a deputy overman, of 24, Pendower Way, Pendower Estate, Newcastle.

The injured, now in Newcastle Infirmary, are:—

Albert Benn (55), of 45, Cochran Street, Newcastle (general injuries); and

William Hepple (44), of 11, Sunnybank Avenue, Benwell (back injury).

Mrs. Scott, the deputy's widow, has now suffered two losses in the pits. A son, Adam Scott, was killed at the age of 30 six years ago near where his father died to-day, and another son, Frank, was injured in an accident in the Montagu Pit a year ago and has been unable to work since.

FRANK SCOTT.

Adam Scott's death six years ago was the last fatal accident in the Charlotte Pit until to-day.

To-day a fall of stone had occurred in the main haulage road and about 12 men were clearing away the debris when another fall took place, burying Scott, Benn and Hepple.

The Evening Chronicle news report on the death of Frank Scott, killed in the Charlotte Pit.

This photo of Linda Sutton (nee Scott) was taken at West End Library on Condercum Road at one of our West Newcastle Picture History Collection group meetings. Linda is interested in finding out about the mining community as some of her ancestors were part of that era.

Precious Memories
by Joyce Vasey

My father, Rowland Vasey, met my mother, Mildred Urquhart, when mum was aged sixteen; they were both good swimmers and they met at Elswick pool. They married when she was nineteen. Dad then went off to war, was captured and made a prisoner for four years. He escaped to Switzerland and eventually returned home.

I was born in 1945 at 32 Clara Street and was one of four children, my siblings are Alexander, Kathleen and Christina. We had a front room which we were only allowed to go in to watch children's TV. When my mam went up to the Terrace shopping and my dad was tinkering about on the car, I used to invite kids into our house, fill our bath and charge them one penny to duck their heads in the water wearing my new bath hat. Most of the time we played games in the street such as "I Bogs" (We looked into the shops window displays and shouted I Bogs for the things we liked, but no one had any money so it became a competition to Bogs first.)

My mother was a dressmaker and she made beautiful wedding dresses for the local brides. I remember that she used a treadle operated Singer Sewing Machine. She continued sewing until a couple of years before she died, even though she was crippled with arthritis. I remember how she made me and my cousin Yvonne dresses from a parachute, we wore them one day to go down to my dad's allotment where he had a shed. He kept a big can of tar on a shelf, we took it down and decided to paint the shed for him, there were yellow marks all over our dresses and our skin. My mam had to use one pound of butter to get the marks off our skin and prize our eyelids apart.

I went to St Columba's Mission and was confirmed at St James' Church where I was also christened and married; I held the bible I was given at confirmation at my wedding. When I was a kid I attended St Columba's three times each Sunday. My mam gave me three pence to put in the collection plate, I used to put the three pence in for the first service and take two pence out to enable me to put one penny on the plate for each of the following services at 11.00 am and at 6.00 pm.

This photo of Clara Street was taken when Joyce was four years old. She is with her Aunt Peggy, her mother's sister. Joyce is wearing a cotton dress and wellingtons.

My granddad had a horse, called Silver, and a cart. He sold coal, fruit and ice cream around the Benwell and Elswick areas. My nana and granddad lived at 72 Clara Street and in winter she came down the street carrying a bucket of cinders. She scattered them on the ice in front of her so that she could walk down the street safely, as the street was so steep. After visiting us, she would carry on to the Hydraulic Crane to meet her friends for a gill. She always left the bucket in a garden at the bottom of the street.

Children used their sledges to go for messages for the old folks in the street. At night time we warmed our nighties in the black lead oven. We sat in the kitchen to listen to plays on the wireless as it was always warm in there.

My dad worked at a foundry on Scotswood Road and after each nightshift he used to call at the crumpet factory to buy some for our breakfast. I still love crumpets to this day. At the South Benwell School reunion, whilst talking with my friend, I discovered that her father sold the crumpets to my dad all those years ago. Dad also had an allotment where he grew flowers and leeks. He won so many prizes for his leeks and the shows were always an important event in our house. After the show we always had a big pan of soup on the stove.

Dad was a member of the Joan Street Working Men's Club where women were only allowed in on Sunday evenings. Every year, the members had a trip to Redcar or Doncaster races where a good time was had by all. At Christmas, the members' children were taken to a pantomime. We each received an orange and a half a crown (about 15p in today's currency) it was a lot of money in those days.

Every Saturday we bought lovely meat pies from Mrs Foggo and then we got the chips from the fish shop where Sidney Robson's mother worked.

I attended South Benwell School until 1959 when everyone was sent to Atkinson Road School where I stayed for one year and left school aged fifteen. I started work at Scottish and Newcastle Breweries as a punch card operator in the offices on Claremont Road. Eventually we moved to the computer section at the Gallowgate Offices. When I was fifteen I used to spend some of my pay on seamed stockings, but then tights came

South Benwell School pals with their teacher. Back row, left to right: Connie Pegg, Brenda McGowan, M. Lynn, Caroline Cox, Yvonne Ward, Mrs Clark. Front row: Sandra Nicholson, M. Shillinglaw, Jean Symons, Joyce Vasey, Brenda Grant, Florence Maddock and Pat Dawson.

into fashion. On opening my first pair of tights I discovered that there were three legs instead of two, what was I to do, cut one off and go around with a hole in them, I was in a hurry to go out and didn't have time to take them back.

The Easter Bonnet Parade from the Hydraulic Crane pub shows Joyce's grandmother, Tilly Urquart, wearing a hat made from masks. Tilly is standing next to Sylvia Kirk wearing flowers on her hat.

I was married in 1966 and my husband Albert Willis and I moved to 244 Buddle Road. We used to borrow a six foot tin bath from my mam's house at 300 Buddle Road, we filled the bath from a geezer, although it took a long time to fill it. It was most enjoyable having a bath in front of a coal fire. On one occasion my husband was returning the bath to my mam's when he heard music from the Joan Street Club. He was intending to have a pint after he returned the bath, however, he carried on straight into the club with the bath on his back. He was struggling to get it through the door when the doorman came to his assistance. Once inside the foyer, the doorman asked why he was bringing a bath into the club, Albert was most embarrassed and quickly left the club to return the bath to mam's house. The bath was stolen some weeks later, and that was the end of bath nights in front of the fire.

My parents moved to West Denton in 1969. At last they had a house with central heating and a bath!

We still laugh at a family story, when my nana and granddad went to Blaydon on their horse and cart. My nana was holding my mam, who was a baby, in her arms, when it started to rain. She looked at the baby and shouted to my granddad "Alex, my bairn's bleeding!" Then they both noticed that in the rain, the red feather from my nana's hat was dripping onto the baby's face.

We moved to Wardley in 1969 and our first baby Debra Louise was born in 1970. We moved back to Newcastle in 1973 where our second daughter Julie Allison was born, and in 1975 we were on the move again to Hastings, East Sussex, where Albert was Chief Accountant for the local council. He subsequently became Treasurer and Deputy Chief Executive for Rother District Council.

Joyce as she is today at home in Hastings. She visits Newcastle every year and says that her heart is still here in Newcastle.

When the children were old enough, I worked as a doctor's receptionist until I retired in 2006. We are now both retired and we are kept busy looking after our five grandchildren. We always look forward to returning to Newcastle every year to visit friends and family. My childhood memories of life in Newcastle are precious to me.

The Lamplighter
by Sarah Burn

Sarah (née Mullen) Burn was christened in St Aidan's Church in 1916. Her grandmother, Mary Simpson, lived at No 61 St John's Road in a house which was directly opposite the cemetery. Sarah is known as Sadie by everyone. Her siblings were James Frederick born in 1920 and Harold born 1923 who was a 'Good dancer'. She attended Canning Street School and remembers that Mr John McKenna was one of the teachers there and Mr Jones was the head master.

"He was a good pianist, a good teacher and strict. I got the strap for putting a piece of chalk down my sock. I daren't tell my mam when I got home or I would have been in more trouble from her. My dad just had to give us kids one of his looks and we knew how far to go. We never stepped out of line when he gave that look."

Sadie Burn at her care residence in Burnopfield.

On the subject of punishment, Sadie remembered her grandmother Mary: "She was strict, I suppose she had to be with five girls and four boys to look after. If anyone got into trouble she'd reach for her slipper. Once, me and Cybil were playing a game of rides on each other's back, I slipped and my elbow went through the window of the police station which was opposite my grandmother's house. We both ran and hid in her toilet in the back yard. Cybil said: 'That's it! You'll have to pay for it.' But we need not have feared because the policeman covered for us and said that it was an accident."

The Methodist Church at the top of Condercum Road was where Sadie went as a child, but she wasn't impressed there: "They would stamp your card and they locked us in so that we couldn't dodge back out." Sadie still keeps the Temperance certificate which her grandmother was asked to sign in 1895.

Tom Mullen, a street lighting inspector. His job was to ride around the streets checking that all lights were in working order. He would climb a ladder to replace a gas mantle if he found that the light had gone out.

Friends of Sadie's in Benwell were Peggy Fairhurst and Sybil: "There used to be a church procession which met in the car park of the Majestic Cinema. We'd go along Condercum with Peggy holding the banner, down Atkinson Road, then along Buddle Road up St John's and back along Gill Street – we got an orange. We liked to go on the Terrace (Adelaide Terrace) – Nichol Reay had an ice cream shop, it was the best you had ever tasted, but he would never give away the recipe, it went with him when he died. We used to buy a Rizzi, they were so big you couldn't get them into your mouth. He also used to go around the streets in winter with hot chestnuts."

Sadie's father James Frederick was born in Rachel Street; he had been in the territorials. He became a lamplighter inspector. It was his job to go around on a motorbike with sidecar and make sure that the gas lights were on. He was knocked down by a drunken car driver and was never quite the same. He died young in his 50s. Her mother was a good cook but she would never attempt to make Christmas cake, Sadie was always given that job.

Her Aunt Ethel Lived in Theodosia Street in

full view of the grave yard, it was the first place she saw as she stepped out of her door. Ethel's husband used to joke that if she popped her clogs, she would just be rolled to the cemetery.

There were corner shops everywhere and one shop in particular that Sadie recalls was Scott's on the corner of Colston Street: "Frank and Doris ran the shop, I can still see him now in his brown dust coat, when you went into the shop, he'd say about his wife "She's at it again, always washing clothes, if I come back in another life I'm going to be a clothes horse."

Wesley Hall
BAND OF HOPE

I promise to abstain from all INTOXICATING LIQUORS as beverages
Signed Sarah Simpson
Nov 11 1895 Sec C Mattison

THE NEWCASTLE, GATESHEAD & DISTRICT BAND OF HOPE UNION

A Temperance Certificate. People were required to sign this statement to promise to abstain all alcohol.

Sadie was married in 1938 to Tom Burn in St James' Church and she remembers that the sleeves of her dress came to a point at the cuff: "Grandma Burn took it up as it was too long, I kept it for years and then a dress was made out of it for our Eileen, my daughter. Eileen was born in 1946 and died in 1986."

Soon afterwards, Tom joined the RAF, he didn't wait to be called up and was keen to serve. Peggy Fairhurst's husband was also in the RAF and they were firm friends. Sadie and Tom also had a son Tom who was born at No 102 Condercum Road. He went to Canning Street School also and by this time Mr McKenna had become the headmaster. He passed to go to Rutherford Boys' School. Tom also went to Scott's shop, just as his mam had done and he said: "I spent my pocket money in there. There were sweets and the biscuits were kept in tins behind the counter; they had cakes on the counter in glass jars. I remember they had a machine that sliced the ham. I used to love those Jubilee's, a kind of triangle shape on all sides, but not a pyramid, they were lovely, but made your hands cold."

HOLY BAPTISM

Benwell Parish Church.
NEWCASTLE-ON-TYNE.

The Child of
Was baptized on
In
Signed

A certificate of Baptism for James Frederick Mullen which was presented by St James Church.

Sadie enjoyed thinking about her old haunts: "I'd go back down to Condercum Road tomorrow to live, but I know that it's not the same now. I remember that there was a fruit shop at the top of Hugh Gardens, there was a wash house on Bond Street, Jennings Bakery was opposite what is Adelaide House now. We used to go to Mallaby's, they sold everything in there, it was a huge shop, it stood where the Search Project is now. Our Tom used to get his Mechano bits, they sold wireless sets and we also bought the sash cords for the windows. Storey's hardware shop was at the top of Clara Street. The cinema, the Grand Palace was run by Irene Boakes' dad. If it was full he'd say "Everybody move up, two on a seat please."

Tom visits his mam Sadie regularly taking her chocolates and flowers. She now lives in Burnopfield and has lovely views across the valley towards Rowlands Gill. As we look out of the window, a pair of rooks peck at the grass and a pheasant forages for food, but Sadie still thinks of her life in Benwell and says that she would much prefer looking out onto the busy traffic and people busying around. "I once went up the Grey's Monument and saw brilliant views."

A Local Lad
by John Buchan

John was born in 1931 and has lived in Benwell for 48 years. He is married to Audrey and his mother was Mary (née Gaffon), father Tom, with siblings Olive and Robson.

"I was eight years old when war broke out and my mam asked me if I wanted to stay at home or go with the others during evacuation. I chose to stay at home and there were only half a dozen of us who stayed. We could hear the bombs going off, and I particularly remember the one at Blaydon – Adams brick works – it was a noisy time. We used to go around the streets picking up pieces from shells and bombs. There was also a bomb went off at the top of Hampstead Road, a dentist lived there, but I don't know if anyone was injured. The council sent an Anderson Shelter to our house."

"We went to the cinemas, there were so many that we could see a different film every night. We went to Rye Hill, the Rialto, the Rex and the Embassy. There used to be a one on Adelaide Terrace which used to be a car component place before. We played football mostly, but I enjoyed playing a game called Jack Shine Your Light. If one of us had a torch, he would send us all to hide, then seek us out shining the torch around. We also didn't mind playing skippys with the lasses. There's too much time spent on computers now, the kids aren't as fit as we were. We had our seasons for which games we played, there'd be liggys or marbles, but we had other names for them like pinkies or glass alleys – they were the shiny ones with bonny colours inside."

John Buchan at home as he looks through old photos and shares his memories of the barrage balloons and the sounds of the bombs during the war.

"Your mother had a set routine for her housework: Monday for washing, Tuesday for ironing, Wednesday she would bake and so on."

I worked at Vickers Armstrong as a coppersmith, forty-eight hours a week, the whole factory was very noisy. We made boilers, they were riveted then, not welded.

The last night in the Benwell House pub – known as Lambies for many years. Left to right: Ray Wharton, Eric Johnson, John Wilson, Charlie ?, Ray Smith, Mattie Bryson, Davie Hall, Walter ? and Jimmy Cartman (manager)

I used to go to the Bond Street dance when I was about sixteen. It was only coppers to get in and all of the musicians were blind. It was also used as a swimming baths, but when the dance was on they would put a false floor over the top. There used to be a dance on Atkinson Road, just opposite the Carnegie Library – the building had been used as the British Legion and then for the Boys' Brigade. It's been pulled down for years now and nothing is there in its place yet.

Just where the old clinic used to stand on Atkinson Road, that's where the barrage balloon site used to be. They put them there to stop the enemy aircraft from flying in low or landing. A high wind dragged the balloon from its base and it knocked the top off the steeple from St James' church.

Just past Hodgkin Park Road there was a pub, we called it Lambies, but I think it was the Benwell House, at the bottom of Pendower. I was there with my mates for the last drink before it was closed to be reopened as a funeral parlour. The manager made us all laugh when he said: "You're aal standing here drinkin' tonight, but yis could be lying here tomorrow!"

"I went to war, like everyone else I knew, I was stationed in Kenya. When I came back I got a part time job at the Majestic Cinema as a handyman. When it rained we had to get up onto the roof from the outside to get inside the loft. I was in there to move the chandelier and I put my foot through the ceiling. It wasn't as grand as the one in the episode of *Only Fools and Horses* where Del and Rodney send it crashing to the floor.

Lizzie Grant, a performer at the Majestic Theatre looks grand in her principal boy costume.

"I used to run a youth club in the parish hall; the other lads were Brian Smithson, Dennis and John. There used to be football and table tennis, no set thing, just whatever the kids wanted to do – that was in the 1960s."

"I married Audrey Kilpatrick, she was born along Forth Banks. We have two sons – John, born 1955, he works at the RVI Hospital and Alan, born 1957, is a caretaker. He was the youngest one to work for the council. They both went to Atkinson Road School. Audrey goes to the Bingo and when she's due to come back, I go to the top of the street on Adelaide Terrace to go and get her."

The Majestic when it was a theatre in 1929 when the Denville Stock Company played there.

A Lifetime of Books
by Des Walton

When Des Walton knew that I was interested in local history and a member of the West Newcastle Picture Collection group, he was eager to talk about his memories. He invited me to his home in Nunsmoor Road and we spent a couple of hours looking at old photos, books and maps.

"I discovered Elswick Library as a kid and joined."

Des started work as a junior librarian at Fenham library and when the Second World War started all of the male staff were called up. He was in the navy as a telegraphist, travelling to places such as West Africa, India, Burma and Ceylon. He helped sink some U-boats in the Atlantic and spent most of the war in the Indian Ocean.

"I was torpedoed by the Japanese, but I got away with it."

Des posing with his precious books

Des was demobbed back to Newcastle in 1946 and went to work in Scotswood Library. He remembers learning about the Montagu Pit disaster and helped to make slides for the archive.

"I became interested in the Scotswood Pit, Montagu pit, it had various names. I was the specialist on the history of it. I taped the stories from the men and some of them were living in Westerhope. I also worked in West Denton Library and we took on the outer west.

"There were gardens built next to the church to remember the men. I met some of the men who had escaped. There is a photo of me and Jimmy Forsyth taken with two of the men, brothers. It was taken in the school on Atkinson Road. I met Jimmy in 1954 when he came to the library to sell some of his photos. When Jimmy walked in the door, I didn't know that he had taken so many photos. He was a Welshman with one eye, he became interested in the history of Elswick and started to buy a whole lot of stuff, maps, books etc. He had worked at ICI Prudhoe, he'd only been there three or four days when a piece of metal flew into his eye. Jimmy couldn't go back to Wales, he'd had a small job in a factory, a fitter before then."

The members of the history group in the old Benwell Library on Atkinson Road. Des Walton is on the left, Warren Thompson (standing) and Jimmy Forsyth (right). The group started life as West Newcastle Local Studies.

Des said that everyone in the library knew Jimmy and he was always bringing new photos in: "As we looked at them, I realised that he had captured the whole ending of that industrial society, the crumbling and demolition of the buildings and most importantly, the people. I asked him if he would mind if I took copies of them to start up an archive of the photos and he brought all of his negatives and handed them over for us to borrow.

"I got to work with my team and we worked hard to develop and record everything. Jimmy wasn't interested in the negatives, all he wanted was to take photos. It took up a huge part of my life. We sought professional advice on how to get contact prints of negatives, then we stuck them onto cards and wrote the information alongside. An assistant was paid to catalogue them, but the funding dried up.

"When I was talking to people I used to borrow their photos and copy them. I retired 24 years ago and have spent my days doing this and also adding all the suburbs of Newcastle. We formed an organisation with Phil Kitchen, a community worker, who was based at Arthur's Hill and Elswick Local History Society was formed. But there was a risk of fire so he suggested that we move the collection to City Library to build up the collection. Then Fred Millican joined us. Fred and I used to go around talking to folks. We went to the church to talk to the vicar."

"I've written about seven Bygone books, two personal ones including Bygone Westgate Road." As he leafs through one of them he recalls: "I'm looking for a photo of an old cart, I think it's in one of the Westgate books, it reminds me of the ice cream carts that came around the streets, Eldorado Ice Cream. Stop me and buy one. There's a book by Jonathan Priestman on the Glue Factory and Tannery in 1843. Benwell didn't become part of Newcastle until 1904. The factory closed in the 1860s, there was a rapid decline of tanning. There used to be an abattoir situated between the Pipe Track Lane and Violet Street, it opened in the 1940s/50s when cattle were drove through the streets to the cattle market at Marlborough."

He remembered a local entertainer, Des has a draft of his book: "Jimmy Muir was a well known raconteur. He went around concert parties and I remember laughing at him in the 1930s, then I met him as someone who was living in Benwell. I discovered that he had written a book and had been promised that it would be published. It was called Newcastle's Victorian Townships and there is lots on Benwell in it. Also a section on South Benwell School. I provided him with copies of photos of the area, but he decided that he wanted the book to be more like a personal family history, of living in Benwell all his life, and it wasn't printed. It was a 100 page manuscript typed by himself on his 1917 typewriter. He also painted in oils and watercolours, was a local historian and comic. He worked for the old Tyne Improvements Commission for forty five years, but was still an after dinner entertainer. He used to say "I hope I live long enough to see the end of Coronation Street."

Des is also working on his family history with relatives. He is still very much involved in the history of Newcastle and has visitors calling on him to share his expertise on all sorts of subjects. He would love to be more involved with local groups and is available for advice on times gone by. He's like a mini Google.

Mike Greatbatch, Heritage Interpretation Officer, and Des Walton at the official opening of the new West End Library.

From Ireland to Benwell
by Lawrence O'Brien

Peter Joseph O'Brien used to go into a shoe shop in Bray, County Wicklow when he was around nine years old. He learned a little about shoe repairs then. He first moved from Ireland, from Dunleavy to Holyhead on the mail boat, he left his mother and four sisters behind.

"He always said that he would have went straight back the next day if he'd had the fare," says Lawrence, his son. "He went to Wales, then to Coventry, where he was married in the Cathedral. He worked in a munitions factory in Coventry where he met my mam, she was from Newcastle. They came back here when my mam was expecting her first child, they lived with grandparents in Fenham. My dad worked for a cobblers in Gosforth at first and mam worked in Tilley's Café in town. Dad had also worked as a doorman at the Irish Club in town. Our Eileen lived on Amelia Walk, she lived on one side and her son lived on the other."

When Lawrence was a lad he remembers the trolley buses: "When the driver approached Ferguson's Lane the lever had to be switched so that the bus could change to another track. Me and a couple of my pals would shout 'It's ok, we'll switch it for you.' The driver would shout back 'Thanks lads.' Then we wouldn't do it and run away when the bus stopped. The rods on top of the bus would bounce about in all directions. The driver waved his fist at us and then had to get off the bus to fetch a pole, which was kept just under the bus at the side, it was nicknamed 'The Frog' for some reason. The pole was hooked onto the rods one at a time to attach them to the line again, then off he would go."

Lawrence remembers that his dad used to ride on a bike: "He rode all over the place to pick up shoes, he even picked up the army boots from the barracks in the 1950s. He took over the shop on Farndale Road in 1963 and I worked with him, mam also helped in the shop. It was called Asnew Shoe Repairs. He mended the shoes in the cellar part and sister June lived in the upstairs flat – June was married in 1971 at St Bede's. He

A crashed trolley bus lies on its side on Benwell Lane in 1959.

worked in the shop until he was 65 years of age. I think back to when he used to work in the garden shed, he repaired the shoes for all the friends and neighbours. But, he always kept the fare back to Ireland, he always made sure that he had the money ready if he ever needed it."

Sister June says that Lawrence is known locally as Paddy, as he's got Irish blood: "They all know him as Paddy the Cobbler. He still travels around to pick up shoes from different places. He goes to George's Hardware shop on Chapel House on Tuesdays and fetches them back by Friday."

Lawrence O'Brien who is known locally as "Paddy" in his shop Asnew Shoe Repairs on Adelaide Terrace.

Lawrence is a member of the Springbank Social Club and is a popular figure in the community and many the time I've called in there and he is sharing memories with Benwell people. I met John Hunter there, he lives in Shafto Court. We were remembering locals and John spoke of Sammy McClusky: "He always looked after his wavy hair. He used to pop out to the shop for a bottle of beer every Sunday to wash his hair – he said it kept it in good condition. He was always immaculate and if a new suit came out today, he had it tomorrow. He used to go away working in the pubs and clubs in Bognor Regis and back here in the winter."

John Hunter used to live in Amelia Street, Benwell and worked as a machine operator at Vickers. He spoke of the social clubs: "The beauty of it was that everybody had their own club where you walked in and they said 'Hello'. Mine was the Joan Street Club. Everybody held a leek show and afterwards we made a huge pan of broth and ate it with a lump of bread. When we went out on a Saturday night, we came back, put the gas mantle on and the blacklocks were everywhere, hundreds of them. I used to enjoy it when I was a kid because I could knock them out with a shovel."

John Hunter, a customer of Lawrence's who lives at Shafto Court.

Lawrence keeps shoes that haven't been collected after he has repaired them and sells them for £1 to anyone who may be interested. Good to see that recycling is still alive and kicking, and that there's always a customer or two in there ready to tap out a tale or two.

Springbank Social Club

Manny Miller became a member of the Springbank Social Club in 1953 and for many years was at the helm of the club. Even in retirement he continues to help out. He explained that the club started in the Benwell Assembly Rooms, it had been a snooker hall, then a Bingo and then Gibson's Fruit Shop. Members who went to the Assembly Rooms borrowed money from London Victoria Insurance Company which was situated at the top of Clara Street back then. They used the money to buy the building at the top of Condercum Road. In pre-war days, the Salvation Army sang and played their music in the grounds. Then in more recent times, the jazz bands performed there. Manny was told that the building had been owned previously by Brims the builders and shipyard people and also by a dentist.

He points out two group photos showing ex-committee men, one is from the 1920s, another photo shows the men sitting in smart suits with the gardens of the club in the background. There are certificates to show their achievements. Throughout the club there can be seen many local scenes and Jimmy Forsyth photos.

The main entrance of the Springbank Club. They now have a purpose built shelter for smokers which houses three heaters and lighting which activate the moment a clubber walks in.

Registered No. R6848. Northumberland.

BENWELL & DISTRICT SOCIAL CLUB & INSTITUTE, LIMITED.

THE FIRST

Annual General Meeting

Will be held upon the

CLUB PREMISES,

on

SUNDAY, MAY 30th, 1920.

Chair to be taken at 10-30 a.m. prompt.

BUSINESS.

1.—Chairman's Remarks.
2.—Minutes of the last General Meeting.
3.—Adoption of the Balance Sheet and Accounts.
4.—Consideration of Officers' Salaries.
5.—Appointment of Scrutineers.
6.—Any other Business according to Rule.

J. DOUGHERTY,
Chairman.
J. LEVEY,
Secretary.

J. Dowling & Sons, Ltd., Printers, Station Road, Whitley Bay.

The first annual general meeting of the Springbank Social Club was held in 1920 and the club still keep the agenda. It is on display in the manager's office.

Bruce Tinsley: "I put myself up for election to be a committee man about twelve years ago. Before that I was working in Bookless at the warehouse, just along the road, Lisle's garage was opposite the water company cottage which is called Fenham Cottage. I used to call in to this club for a drink, it was near to where I worked, it was handy, that was in 1981. Then I joined the club."

Manny lived in Homeland on Hodgkin Park and his cousin Tommy Miller lived near the bottom of Maughan Street. The first school Manny attended was Elswick Road and then he went to Pendower Technical School: "It was just for lads then, but later became a school for girls.

"I joined as a committee man in 1964, then, became Vice Chairman, then Chairman, Treasurer and eventually Secretary from 1973/4 until 2009. We've always had turns at the club, singers and comedians, Bobby Thompson used to perform here. Back then the lounge was the concert room and they only used a microphone, nothing like the high fives that they use now. It was always really busy – Fridays was dance night and full just about every other night too, so much so that we had a new concert room built in 1972. There were actually Roman ruins under there, but there wasn't time to excavate. The club's name derives from the fact that a stream ran under the building, It is supposed to run right down to the river."

He compared the prices from back then when it was 50p to get in. Today the cost is £2, but good value for entertainment and reasonably priced drinks.

This photo of Manny Miller (left) was taken in the bar of the Springbank Social Club on Condercum Road. Manny is sitting with Peter Scorer.

The Springbank is not only used for entertainment acts: "We have a football team which is doing very well. They provide their own coaches to matches, they are self sufficient and use the club as a base. We also have a fishing club, a bowling club that plays at Leazes Park and a darts team which plays in the bar. Years ago women weren't allowed in the bar but that's all changed now. The women usually choose not to go in there because we often have working men who call in wearing their working clothes – it's more casual in there for the men."

There has also been both Jolly Girls and Jolly Boys groups at the Springbank. The club is responsible for many fund raising ventures, they have supported groups such as Tiny Lives, Bubble, Happy Days, Cancer Care for Children, the Sarah Marie Fairly Sunflower Memorial Trust among many others and they have certificates to show amounts raised for thousands of pounds.

"When the Old Hall Social Club and the Joan Street Club closed – the area was being demolished – many of their members came up here. But the area lost a lot of local people as some moved away to Blakelaw and all over the place, so it's a bit like swings and roundabouts, we gained and we lost."

From left to right, some of the members of the committee at the bar in the lounge. Tommy Hardy, Terry Lisle, Colin Wilkinson, Bruce Tinsley, James Newsome and Tony Jones.

Winters and Christmas Time

The first thing that comes to mind when I recall Benwell winters is calling on a friend: "Aar yi comin' oot ti play?" I daren't knock on the door as I looked up to the gigantic icicles hanging from the roof above, I had no wish to be impaled. As none of the buildings had central heating, their whole structure was extremely cold. Snow built up until it was too heavy, or the slightest increase in temperature, then there'd be an avalanche. This always happened after a housewife had just cleared the path.

As it happened, my friend came to the door: "Naar, me ma 'll not let is oot 'cos the snur's si bad." Then she slammed the door and I just got away in time before half a dozen of the big buggers speared down. It wasn't so bad then, I had a free ice lolly, although it tasted of soot. If there had been anyone else out we could have had a sword fight with them. Back home, it was no better. The net curtains used to stick to the windows from the inside and I regularly got my tongue stuck from trying to lick the ice from the glass. Hands would be numb from snowball fights, then you'd need to rush indoors to warm them at the fire. "Watch, you'll get chilblains!" the old 'uns would say, but we didn't care, it was great to be outdoors.

The streets were the steepest in Newcastle it seemed to us and ideal for sledging with usually an old roller skate with a piece of wood, or a bin lid, depending on how slippy it was. The snow was always piled high along the side of the road covered in soot from the chimney smoke. It was pleasing to put a footprint in it to see the white print below. A real treat was when my mam forgot to get the washing in and a jumper had frozen solid on the line. I crashed it around until it thawed out.

It's difficult to see the numbers of these trolley buses, but judging by the weather, the people would just be glad to be aboard.

At school there was always a long slidy area the full length of the playground. We used to take it in turns to see how far we could get without falling over. Then the caretaker would play the spoilsport and put ashes down. Nowadays, the kids aren't allowed out until all is completely safe, what they are missing out on! I was once shown the boiler room by a friend of mam's who was leaving a message for the caretaker. I can still remember the dry heat and the smell of coke and the brilliant white light of the fire when he opened the massive circle shaped door. But, the most exciting pastime was if I came across a bucket of water with a solid cake of ice on top. I'd be there for ages trying to chisel it out with the heel of my shoe, then belt it with stones to shatter into tiny pieces.

My sledges were always handmade by dad and they were practically designer. He used to hammer strips of metal along the runners so that it would go faster. Everyone admired them and I always passed them on to someone else when I got a new one the next year. One winter, I started off at the top of Maria Street and the sledge really picked up speed halfway down. I lost control and a parked wagon at the bottom loomed large, I had to lie flat on my back still holding on to the rope, travelled straight under the vehicle and out at the other end.

The ashes were always kept to use on the ice in the back yard. There'd be a line towards the outside toilet and the coal house next door. The seat of the toilet always had a sheet of slippery ice over it, and you had to clear it away before sitting down, or you'd be on the floor of the netty. Pipes were forever bursting, so there'd be old rags tied around them which did little to help and they looked appalling.

We sometimes made our own Christmas decorations, sat on the carpet with crepe paper forming them into chains. Mam got up the ladder one year and arranged them in a wheel starting at the rose to the corners and to the outer edges of the ceiling. When dad came in from work, he let the budgie out of its cage. It swung from chain to chain and snapped them all in half. It was around about this time that we realised why the coleus plant was looking threadbare, pretty boy had been at work on that also. Mam always started early with the preparations by paying weekly to save for a hamper. I remember we always got a tinned chicken, she had to open it both ends with a tin opener because it was packed tightly and surrounded by a heavy jelly, then she would poke it out with the bread gully knife. Battenburg cake was in there along with a bottle of Cherry Brandy and Toblerone, tins of cooked meats and sweet mince pies.

I went to St Aidan's church as a Brownie where we played games and sang songs. Every Christmas they held a Fayre and one time mam saved up to buy a dinner service. It was bone china, hunting scenes painted on both inside and out of the cups. It was her pride and joy. She used a Provident ticket to buy a china cabinet, which were all the rage back then, it was a kind of fake ivory coloured marble with silver ribbon designs on the glass. The tea set was displayed inside and never ever used.

Christmas was a great time to top up on my creative resources. I loved painting and those little tins with tiny pans of colour were my favourites; the brushes were very poor quality, there would be little bristles floating around in the water. To go with them I had a couple of colouring books, the paints were very weak and the pale colours would soak through the paper. I'd often use a drinking glass to clean the brush and make the mistake of taking a swig out of it thinking it was my pop glass.

St Aidan's Church taken in 1955 on the Joseph Street side. A Ford Capri is standing outside.

My dad brought a broom shank in from the hardware shop and sawed lots of little discs from it. He painted half of them black and half white, then he painted a draughts board – we used to play for hours. Every year in my stocking there'd be the usual compendium of games, which I hated. They were designed with cards of dobbers and counters which were to be cut out before a game could be played. More often than not I cut through a couple of them making the game defunct from the start. I much preferred my dad's creations. Ludo was one of the games – a little box with a hole in the centre for the counters to fall into once you had plecked them on the corners. The cardboard was of such poor quality, it was only possible to have around a dozen games before the construction caved in, making a mockery of the adverts on the box promising 'Endless fun'. There was never a dice in the compendiums, but instead, one of those spinners which was worked by twirling it with a matchstick through the centre.

My pal Irene asked: "Why did none of the adults suggest that a dice might be better, maybe even buy us one ready before we opened the games? The compendium of games used to have this horse game inside, green, tiny plastic ones with bandy legs. They never stood up properly and used to drive me mad and I wanted to chuck them away, but I still continued to play with them. There'd be a Woolworths exercise book and colouring pencils, but you kept having to sharpen them as the lead was usually broken all the way down and the tops fell off."

She said: "There were always annuals, I remember getting *The Bunty* and not wanting it. There was a page inside with those paper dressing dolls which had the tags on the shoulders and sides of the clothes. I always forgot when cutting them out and snipped the tags off. We always opened our presents in the morning, but we kept my granny's until later when she came for her tea. I went to my aunties and she gave me an orange, an apple and two shillings piece, it was called a florin then. She would put it all in a brown paper bag with a bar of chocolate and twist it around at the top with a gift tag on."

Adelaide Terrace in 1969 with Woolworths on the left.

The crafts we took home from school were the same every year. For those that could afford Kraft cheese triangles, they could use the round box to fill with plaster of Paris and decorate it before it set with a sprig of plastic holly, a cheap candle and a bit of tinsel. Irene recalled: "Yes, the kids used the plastic holly, but I noticed that the teacher's demonstration piece was always real. We were never given decent candles, they must have been really cheap. There was never a drip down the side like you saw on the Christmas cards, but it would go lop sided with a well of wax in the middle."

We moved from Maria Street when we got the chance of a house. Buddle Road ran through all of the terraced houses which ran down to Scotswood Road. It was more spacious than our last place, two bedrooms, a kitchen and sitting room on the first floor and attics with three bedrooms and a bathroom with an inside toilet! We could do away with the old tin bath, no more plinkety plinking sounds keeping us awake when it rained. I think that mam and dad left the old bath on the nail in the back yard at Maria Street when they left. But the bonus was having a toilet indoors, no more sliding around on an icy seat in the winter. We now owned a boiler which heated the water instead of boiling pans and a kettle on the stove in order to take a bath.

Our new dwelling at No 22 appealed to me as it had a rather grand bannister which I could slide down. There was no stop at the end as it carried on along the landing and then wound around again down the next flight of stairs to the front door. Once outside the front door there were another six concrete steps before we were onto the path. When there had been a thick fall of snow they were a devil to get down. Those old buildings were an impressive sight from the outside, and especially with snow on them, a real picture post card it seemed to me.

When I was about eleven or twelve we bought our first TV set and at first it was a novelty, even watching the test card scene of the little girl surrounded by patterns was exciting. But, I dreaded New Year's Eve, as my mam watched *The White Heather Club* with Andy Stewart. He was dressed in a kilt and sang *The Scottish Soldier* and *Step we Gaily*. The male dancers were in their kilts and the women pranced around in flouncy 1950s short sleeved cotton dresses, even though it was in the middle of winter. They held on to the edge of their skirts and curtsied at the end of a dance daintily in their white high heels and the men bowed. Andy shifting his weight from one muscle bound leg to the other and with a little raise of each shoulder in time to the music, he'd be off singing *Mairi's Wedding* in his little jacket, tartan and furry sporran – "Heel on heel and toe on toe." Then Moira Anderson would appear. I couldn't wait for them to sing *Auld Lang Syne* and then it was finished. He could only have been in his twenties, but to me he seemed ancient.

My husband, David Young remembers Christmas: "We used to sing Gloria, Hosana in Excelsis and we had to hold our breath for the long bit. My sister Carol and me would go to bed and get up in the middle of the night to see what we'd got as presents. Mam and dad were still in bed and we would go to the bedroom to tell them that Santa had been. My mother used to get up, but dad wouldn't, he was still plastered after a night out at the Old Hall where he drank and played cards with his mates.

He helped his mam cook the Christmas dinner, peeling and chopping the vegetables. He said that she made the best roast potatoes and says that this is why he likes cooking now. She would sing to him as they worked *The Little Boy that Santa Claus forgot.*

David said: "I think it was her way of saying that she had done her best for us. Everybody came to our house, Alec and Rene Barclay came for something to eat after the dinner. I don't know how my mam managed because we didn't have much money. Billy and Betty Graham used to live in Benwell, and my dad got him a job delivering pop on the vans. Billy got promoted but moved away to Cudworth Co-op and we put them up for the week. One year, during dinner, my dad was called out on a breakdown, a wines and spirits lorry had overturned in the snow. We had a happy Christmas that year because we had bottles. Word got around and everybody and their granny came to ours, but that's the way my mam was. She had an open house and prided herself in putting out a huge spread.

"They always bought dates, I don't know why because we didn't eat them, they were in my stocking, I always took one bite and spat them out, and we continued to get them year after year. There'd be a bag of mixed nuts, walnuts and almonds mainly, and we could never open them – we had to wait until my dad finally got out of bed. He would crack them ok, but ate half to himself as he went along. Most of our toys were 'Made in Hong Kong' and were broken by the end of the day, but we could read our *Beano* and *Dandy* annuals"

The Youngs always had a real tree. "It was a big tree with lots of decorations, glass baubles, there was allsorts on it – nothing matched, but it didn't matter. My mam enjoyed making her own decorations by spraying bottle tops from Teachers whisky, pine cones and twigs in gold paint, they went on the tree too."

He recalled how lots of wagons got stuck in the deep snow – the coal man and Co-op vans which made regular deliveries – David and his pals would move behind rolling the snow into a giant ball from Buddle Road down to Frank Street, then, when it was around seven feet tall, it would be set free to roll down the steep street.

"The snow lay much thicker back then and the buses had an awful time getting through, and when they did we couldn't see what number it was for the snow which was bleached all over the front windows. Regularly I had to walk to work when a bus didn't arrive, I never thought anything of it."

David Young Snr checking the engine of a van in the Co-op garage.

Bikes, Ponies & Bogies by John James Reid

John was born in 1940 and has lived in a fair few houses when he was growing up in Elswick and Benwell. The first was at 51a Back Glue Terrace and others included 56 Buddle Road, Juliet Street, then back to 51a Back Glue Terrace. He also lived at 45 Hull Street and 16 Jennison Avenue and 204 Condercum Road. Back then, it was easy to obtain an exchange and many families did this for reasons such as to be nearer relatives and for more space when more children were born.

"My dad, James, fought in India during the war. He got on well with all of the different army blokes and taught physical education. He was a sergeant and could have gone to Sandhurst but he turned it down – he didn't want to leave his mates. He met Monty's double and said that there was a strong likeness but he could tell the difference. He came home with an Indian hat, an American hat and shirt. He wore the American clothing when he landed at Southampton and he once got stopped, because it was illegal not to be wearing your own country's uniform. I remember the tales he told of his time in India, especially about the bazaars. One man walked into the market carrying a large attach case, he put it down on the ground, opened it, a man got out, stretched, then got back in by putting his feet to one side. He was then carried away again. He kept us entertained for hours talking about snake charmers and how a monkey could run up a rope. I think because I was told stories, this is how I have a love of writing now. My dad thought that the Indian people were masters of illusion.

John's mam also told the children stories. She was born Mary Ann Carty in 1902 in County Monaghan and she told him that people came from all over the country to Newcastle for work. She was old enough to remember the massive changes that it made to the region. She spoke of the times when the men were demobbed from the army, they all received a suit and new shoes. John's aunt Meggie waited until her husband went out to the pub to take his suit to the pawn shop. Her husband always kept the wardrobe key in his pocket after he had locked the suit and shoes away so Meggie took the back off the wardrobe to get them. Unfortunately, the next day, her husband was due to go to a funeral and the suit wasn't where he had left it.

"Times were hard, in the winter when we ran out of fuel, we started on the furniture for the fire, even cutting doors in half. Mam sent us to jumble sales to buy jumpers, me, our Peter, Roy, Robin, Margaret, Theresa and Sheila. Everyone had a job to do – I was in charge of the poss tub to wash the woollens, someone else would hang them out to dry. Then there was someone to pull the wool out, a couple of us stood with our arms out while someone wound the wool around. Mam knitted the wool back up again

The family of John Reid. Dad, James, the twins Robin and Margaret at the front, John, Theresa and Sheila in the middle and baby Peter held by mother Mary Ann.

to create new clothing for us. Mother's used to act as midwives. If anyone died, they would lay them out. It was sad because if a baby died, there was never enough money to bury them, the cost of a funeral was high. They would wrap the baby up with another body already in a coffin ready for burial."

John attended St Michael's Infants and Junior School. He went earlier than he should have: "I used to winge to be with my sister so they let me in early We got free milk and sat in class with a piece of chalk and a slate. My dad used to say "Education causes brain damage." I also attended Elswick Road and Cruddas Park Schools. I didn't pass my Eleven Plus and from there I went to Whickham View School when we lived at Pendower Estate. I was the captain of both the football and cricket teams. I always enjoyed sport. I had the chance to go to Ireland in 1954. My mam had been in touch with relatives in Ireland, who ran racing stables in County Monaghan. She knew that if it had materialised, dad would have given up work to go with me and lived off the winnings."

John owned a pit pony at the age of fifteen and rigged it up to a cart and friend Donald Gilchrist and another pal were in business. They needed a place to put it out to graze so found a patch of overgrown land on Bentinck Road, took part of the fencing down, then encouraged the pony to go inside. They strapped the pony up to feed but it broke out and came to look for us, running along the cobbles. It kicked the window out of one of the Laws Stores buildings but the police didn't find out.

"I also used to help out at the cattle market. When people bought cattle, it was important to get it away quickly. Cattle often broke out, they could smell death. We used to chase it back. One day a man approached us at the market carrying a piglet in a cardboard box with the intention of selling it. He asked us if we'd take it to an address in Lobley Hill. I'm sitting on the handlebars of a butcher's bike with this pig in the box and when I went to knock on the door of the house, the pig made a break for it. It was a devil of a job to catch it. Then we had to take the poor little thing back with us."

John remembered that his mam baked nedin cakes: "They were a flatter version of a stottie cake, made with plain flour with currants in. They were about ten inches by twelve inches across. They were cut into six so that we could have a piece each. Sometimes we could all have a jam sandwich with no butter, we loved to swap, even though we all had the same thing. You kept in with the butcher, the coal man, everyone, so that you got bigger portions. I remember when anyone went into the

The old Cattle Market.

butcher's shop and asked: "Have yi got a sheep's heed?" and the butcher replied: "Nar, it's just the way my hair's falling doon."

"We had nowt but we had fun, we had nothing to compare things with. I used to make my own bogey. I used to go to the market for potato boxes, get an old pram and mount the axle on a piece of wood. To drill the holes I used a poker which was used to stir the coals on the fire."

John spoke of the working men in the area: "There were miners and the industrial workers, all hard strong men. They arranged boxing matches, there'd be bets made. Sometimes matches were arranged in someone's back yard with a toot on the back door that would raise the alarm if the law was nearby." John remembers when the loser staggered out into the lane, someone would shout: "Right, now, you can carry your bottom lip home on the wheelbarrow."

John credits his enthusiasm to his upbringing in Benwell and says that the start he had there gave him the motivation to try everything. He has had 153 poems printed in the Evening Chronicle and if anyone asks him, he can pen a verse to suit the occasion. He has a lifesaver's certificate, stock car driver's license for formula 1 and 2 racing, is a blood donor, member of the Elders' Council at Mea House and interviews folks on a local radio show on gardening. John grows many plants and gives advice to callers, he grows shark fin melons for friends Wing Wing and Amanda Chan. A group of students made a DVD of John's creations for their degree work in Media Studies. They took photos of his two grapevines and followed him around the shows he attended. He won prizes of £145. John jokes: "The only thing is, you can't grow money!"

He describes his delight at seeing a dog fox coming regularly to his allotment at Moorside where he feeds it sweetcorn.

He has enjoyed working on motorbikes and at one time owned one so quick that John jokes: "It was so fast it caught pigeons." He took part in scrambles, grass track events, trials, hill climbs and he also took up the same activities in cars. He was also a member of a vintage motorcycle club.

John also spoke of when he owned a 1936 Austin 7 in 1963: "It had a sun roof an electric starter, wipers and a spare wheel carrier at the back. A tiny arm which slid along brought a shield down to cover the back. Oh yes, it was a delux model, it had four wheels ... one on each corner. I remember using the L plates, it stood for Look out Lunatic." He laughs.

John is as busy as he has always been, he recently completed a course on dementia, obtaining six certificate passes. He is involved in voluntary work for West End Befrienders. When I speak to John, he is enthusiastic, passionate and totally committed to his work throughout the community. I get the impression that he will be still firing on all engines in everything he does until he is 100 years old, and he certainly has the energy to reach that age.

"I enjoy working on the Elders' Council. It's for older people working together for older people. I just like helping folks."

One of John Reid's bikes with sidecar.

Lucky Legs
by Gary Hogg

As a lad I always had skinny legs. No amount of bike riding or football ever put meat on them. I still have the same legs: Lucky legs.

"Lucky they divven't snap," my brother would say.

"Yer knees is like knots in cotton," my mother would say.

I was blessed with family that wasn't big on adulation.

There was however, a brief spell when I developed calf muscles the size of footballs. It was during my days as a delivery boy in Benwell.

My other brother took over as manager of Thompson's Red Stamp Stores on Adelaide Terrace. I was ecstatic when he told me that he needed a new delivery boy. I already had a paper round but getting the chance to ride a real delivery bike was on a par to being a Telegram Boy on a BSA Bantam. The fact that Benwell was built on the side of a mountain was never mentioned.

At the time, I lived on a posh new council estate in Benton which was flat. I went to school in Heaton which was almost flat. Benwell was something different.
That first journey, upstairs on the number 1, was quite memorable. A large woman with lots of bags squashed me against the steamed up window. There was an unnoticeable climb out of town and the driver staying in a low gear must have gone unnoticed too. We started to pass smoke-blackened terraces split by black cobbled streets. Boarded up windows, peeling paintwork, derelict houses, demolished houses. Yet people still living in the one next door. I'd been to Glasgow as a young child and witnessed the Gorbles. I'd seen the slums in Eastern Europe on "All our Yesterdays" but hadn't realised that Newcastle had places like that as well.

The bus gathered speed as we whizzed past the colourless landscape. Suddenly it dropped through the gears and I was sure that it would topple over as it turned right up St John's Road and made a run up the hill up past the cemetery. I had been told to get off after it turned a sharp left. I was still recovering from the weight of the large woman on the sharp right, but managed to climb free, race down the stairs and hop off the tailboard. I crossed the Armstrong Road at the Sutton Dwellings, up Hugh Gardens and found the shop with its red and white blind, exactly where I'd been told. Then I met the bike.

Ethel Street cartoon drawn by author Gary Hogg. George Dornan and his family lived above the shop in the photo. George served as a paper boy there. The shop was run by Jimmy and Marie Ormond.

It had obviously been made at Vickers as a prototype for some sort of armoured conveyance. There was no carbon-fibre or aluminium wasted on this beast. The framework was the size and weight of scaffold poles. There was a square frame at the front, presumably designed to mount a bren gun but adapted to hold a wicker basket the size of a skip. The whole thing was painted black apart from the last six inches of the rear mudguard which was white. It was twenty years since we'd had a war, but this bike was still prepared for the blackout. God help any motorist that tried to knock me off. This was the days of the Ford Anglias and the Hillman Minxs, neither of which would've come off best in a collision with this machine.

My first delivery was a four stone bag of potatoes to Noble Street flats. Fifty-six pounds, twenty-five kilos or thereabouts. Almost as heavy as me. As I lifted it into the basket, the bike immediately toppled forward. The back wheel hung in the air momentarily before it swung around and whacked me and the spuds against the shop window, much to the amusement of the shop girls watching from behind the bacon counter, and the gorgeous young lass in the snack bar opposite. I was so embarrassed, but I was saved by the lovely Pam Howe who came and held the back end of the bike down while I repeated the exercise. She kept hold until I had climbed into the saddle and almost counterbalanced the whole affair. Off I went down the snicket through Sutton Dwellings sitting as far back in the saddle as I could. As the hills got steeper I realised that I needed to be even further back or carry lead weights in my pocket because I was in serious danger of going over the handlebars. The brakes were full on all the time but only succeeded in slowing me to a more manageable pace. I found the Noble Street flats and did a neat loop to park the bike facing uphill. Was this an integrity test? Did they know that the flat was on the top floor?

My skinny little wobbly legs made their way back down to find the bike-not there. Half a dozen kids were riding it around a patch of rubble strewn grass. I had to run after them and persuade them to part with it. Luckily they were younger than me, they were good kids, naughty but not malicious. I made a mental note not to wear my grammar school blazer next time though.

Two views of Sutton Dwellings. The pictures are from trade postcards produced by the brickworks – Blythe & Sons of Birtley. In its advertising the brickworks declared: 'Over 1,000,000 A1 Facing Bricks were used in the completion of this contract.'

Wherever I delivered involved a steep climb either on the way there or on the way back. The downhill streets like Maughan, Clara, Frank and Hugh Street all stretched from Adelaide Terrace to, well, the river I suppose if the brakes didn't stop me. Delivering there always involved a fear of going over the handlebars, but was rewarded by an empty bike to pedal back. If however it was delivered to Hampstead or Ladykirk it was a real standing up in the pedals job to get there. If there were two or three to take together it was usually faster to push the bike. But the ride back was as enjoyable as that little lad on the Hovis advert.

A view of the steep streets of Benwell – Carol Young with her mother in Frank Street.

My first winter was a nightmare. There had been snow which had turned into slush then froze solid. I was halfway down Joan Street, approaching the really steep bit when I realised that I had no say in where the bike was going. I slid into a gable end on Pipe Track Lane. I managed to get off the bike but realised that I couldn't move. My crepe soled shoes had no grip whatsoever. I was motionless for a good ten minutes, legs like Bambi, feet desperately trying to stay put while I hung onto the bike. I eventually decided all I could do was to lay the bike down, gather the spilt groceries with the help of some local Samaritans and then slide down the last 100 yards on my bum dragging the box behind me. Luckily the bottom of the box held out until I reached the door. I was then left with the job of crawling back up the street on hands and knees, hanging onto the wall or whatever was available. At one point I contemplated taking my shoes off. I felt sure that my socks would have had a better grip. It took me well over an hour to get back to the shop. They were just closing and I had another three deliveries yet to do. No one offered to help. It was suggested sacks were tied to my feet and I was shoved back out into the cold. It was a late finish that night.

That was one of the few disastrous times though. I met some lovely people on my rounds. Some houses were little palaces with all their hard-won hoppings ornaments proudly displayed, the people were always welcoming.

"It's rations Ma!" a little urchin would shout.

"Howway in pet. D'yi want a glass of pop?" Ma would say, leading me into a flat with no wallpaper or carpets. Wall to wall clotheslines, kids diving into the groceries as I carried them through to the scullery and dad sat next to the range in a vest.
I got to love the West End. I worked all day Saturdays in the shop and learned how to bone bacon, slice it and put out the display in the window. I could bone out a shoulder to provide a "knockle" for soup when requested or bone out a ham for a couple of slices for the more affluent. I got to know folks weekly orders off by heart. Half a stone of potatoes, pound of lard and two pounds of sugar were the start to most lists and I would take a spare quarter of tea in my pocket if I thought they'd forgotten it. Thompson's stood next door to the west wall of Sutton Dwellings. Almost leaning against it, apart from a little dog leg snicket that ran in between. The shop was knocked down shortly after I left and there was a bare patch where it had stood for the next few years. I see that Sutton Dwellings has disappeared as well now, with a new set of flats in their place. And the snack bar, I never did get to chat up that gorgeous lass. I did pluck up the courage to go in and buy a pie one day. It was my first experience of a hot Dickman's pie. And my first experience of scalded mouth, chin and neck as I casually bit into it. I didn't dare look back to see if the gorgeous lass had witnessed that as well.

With my first wages I went to the electrical shop further up Adelaide Terrace and bought the new Monkees album and then over the road for a saveloy dip to enjoy while I spent the lunch hour staring at my new record. My second wage packet bought me a pair of Wranglers parallels and the skinny legs were seen no more.

I Loved My Old House by Lilian Pickard (née Owens)

Lilian was born at Violet Street in 1947. She was told by her father that it was reported in the *Evening Chronicle* as one of the worst winters: "He had to dig his way to the midwife's house making tunnels on each side and he said 'My perfect day, but the worst ever winter.' The woman who dad called on was called Dolly, she delivered everybody's bairns. She kept a huge barrel in the yard to catch rain water. She always used to say, 'Never wash your hair in proper tap water.' I once went to Dolly's place, she had an upstairs flat, and at the back there were stone stairs down to the back yard. From that angle I could see right into the barrel, it was full of this horrible green water teeming with life, and this is what she used for her hair."

Lilian went to South Benwell Infants and Juniors, her elder sisters Yvonne and Pat were in the seniors and she remembers crying to be with them, she could see them playing from the yard. When the Seniors' section was closed down, they were all transferred to Atkinson Road School. South Benwell had previously been known as Cox's School after a previous headmaster. Her mother, who was born in 1912, also attended South Benwell: "Mrs Clark, one of our teachers from South Benwell, came with us. She had her favourite girls, I was one of them. I used to babysit for her, she never paid me, but I was taken to the cinema and on trips out."

Lilian could remember a couple of shops in the area: "There was Storey's and Coffee's and also a doll's hospital. Me and our Yvonne had a boodie doll each, mine was dressed in blue and Yvonne's in pink. The arm came off mine, the arms were held on by bits of elastic. Mam took it to the hospital, a teddy of mine was taken there for a set of new eyes. If a doll was broken beyond repair, people used the bits of china in the bottom of plant pots for drainage. Now if a toy is broken they just throw it out and buy another one."

She didn't get into trouble often, but on occasion didn't do as she was told. Her mother made toffee cakes and toffee apples and she would lay them out on a tray to sell: "One day, when I was four years old, she said to me 'Don't touch, our Lily!' When her back was turned I put my finger into a cake, it was red hot and burned my finger. She had just taken them out of the oven. I had to wear a big bandage."

On another occasion, after some lad had kicked a football through the window, Lilian's dad had placed a large piece of glass on the bed: "The windows were the sash design and my dad had the putty ready to fix it into place. I was told not to go near it

Mr & Mrs Owens outside their back door in the lane in 1937 – Lilian's mam and dad.

... so I sat on it and it smashed. Even after he replaced it with a new piece, I still couldn't resist pressing my fingers into the putty."

Lilan was playing in Sutton Dwellings with her friend Hazel, playing a favourite game of most children at the time, throwing stones. One morning, Lilian aimed, missed her target and smashed a woman's window, they both ran away as fast as their legs would carry them. She remembered running down Maughan Street: "The houses at the bottom were more like tenements, I went down that street on the way to the Crown Cinema. I used to run down Hannah Street and Scotswood Road back lane and I could see from there that they were higher than our street. My Aunt Sadie lived at 20 Violet Street, my mam's sister's son was Tommy Burns. He had two friends who were also called Tommy – Tommy Howe and Tommy Hudspeth, who lived at the top of Violet Street and my brother Tommy Owens, all born in Violet Street and inseparable.

Clara Street and Violet Street back lanes were surrounded by allotments. My mam used to save and collect the peelings from potatoes and sprouts, take them up to the allotments and in return she was given rhubarb or a bunch of mint. She made lovely rhubarb pies."

Dennis Pickard, Lilian's husband, acting the goat in Edgeware Road and Hannah Street backlane in 1968.

When Lilian was older, at fourteen, she was fascinated by a neighbour and friend of her aunt who used to pass by. She was a ticket collector for the Elswick Coal Company on Westgate Road: "She took me round with her one day and I loved the way she talked to the customers, went into their houses and collected the money. I went home and said to the family that I was going to have a job like that when I left school. I told them that I was going to call in and ask for a job, they laughed and said that it wasn't possible to just walk in like that. But, that's exactly what I did. By the time I secured the position, the lady had retired. I kept that job for twenty years and I loved every minute of it, it didn't seem like work because I enjoyed meeting the people. They were all good payers. People would ask for a ticket for Farnon's, it was like a sort of white paper cheque with J.J. Supply Co on it. The customers had a payment book which was marked each week. The payments weren't extortionate – if they borrowed £20 they only paid back £21 at £1 per week. If they borrowed £10 they paid back 50p. Mr Heslop who was in charge of the coal company brought the ticket service in for his customers who bought coal from him. They would say to each other ... 'Can you lend me a bucket of coal until mine comes?'

Violet Street during demolition.

After ten years, the £10 and £20 tickets were replaced by £100 as prices in the shops had increased."

Thomas Owens. He had lived in the Munitions Huts after being injured and turned out of the pit cottage in which his family had lived. Thomas managed to take his family away from the huts to live in Gill Street.

Lilian is a keen genealogist and has researched extensively into her family history. She has discovered that her grandfather, William Austin, moved to the region from Westmorland to No 4 School Street. He lived in Benwell and worked on the railways: "When he first came here, he was a Railway Porter." She also found out that her ancestor, Frederick Thomas Dent (Lilian's dad's uncle), died in the Montagu Pit disaster in 1925. Fred had lived at 232 Whitfield Road. A relative, Elsie Hardy helped her with her research by providing photos and information on the family. This excerpt from some of the information: "Fred Dent's body was identified by his brother Luke Dent by his army boots, which were of a heavy pattern. The toe and heel plate were missing, having been worn off. "He had two new ones at home on the chimney piece to put on when he had time" added Luke. Luke Dent showed the coroner a home knitted stocking top with a fancy stitch from which, he said, he recognised his brother's stockings. The witness also recognised his brother's dark body shirt and two decayed eye teeth. Fred Dent's funeral was 27th May 1925 when he was buried with the three who had been recovered with him."

Lilian has learned that her ancestors suffered hard times. Her dad's cousin Mary Ann Owens, aged 21, married Matt Hetherington. They had just married in 1923 and had a baby of nine months of age. Matt was found months later in the arms of his elder brother in the Montagu Pit. They had died like that, locked in each other's embrace and my dad said that they were buried like that at Lemington Cemetery, poor souls."

"My dad's father Thomas Owens lived in Stanley Street. He had an accident in the pit and as he was unable to work and was turned out of the pit house. He was forced to transport his furniture and possessions on a cart along with a wife and six children. In Scotswood, there were munitions huts where people who were down on their luck went. People called them 'The Huts'. Conditions were appalling and they were ashamed to live there – hundreds of people lived there. After a while he managed to take the family away from there and they moved to Gill Street. My Uncle Fred Owens lived at 72 Colston Street."

The Munitions Huts on Scotswood Road. Seen outside is John Robert Dent with Edna Davison. The photo was supplied by Elsie Hardy.

Lilian's dad went to Denton Gardens from there, her grandfather could never work again: "I lived at 35 Hannah Street and I had a singer sewing machine. My friend Hazel was a machinist at a shirt factory at Marlborough Crescent. We used to make clothes at home, Hazel made shirts and I made dresses. I got married in 1967 and moved from Hannah Street and when I watch these housing programmes on TV now which show buildings with all of the original features, I think back, we had all of those in that house. But the powers that be wanted us out, we did get our choice, and we decided on the Fenham area, up the Stamfordham Road. But I loved my old house in Hannah Street."

Teenage Days
by Pat Owens

Pat and her friend Joan Sales (who lived in Frank Street) used to hang around the railway station when they were fourteen years old. The station was across Scotswood Road at the bottom of Frank Street: "Mr Young was the station master, a lovely man, who used to let us sit in the waiting room if it was cold, there would be a great roaring coke fire. We held concerts where we sang all the songs of the day. We ran along the wooden platform towards the signal box, which was more or less at the bottom of Clara Street, then wave up to Dougie Fenwick, the signal man and his young apprentice Steve, who was only sixteen and very good looking. Our June fancied him and we would shout "Can we come up". He would let us if there were no trains due and we were fascinated by the levers and mechanics of it all."

Dougie, Pat's boyfriend, who was later to become her husband.

To the side of the station down an alley, Pat and Joan called in to a factory where they bought mis-shapes: "You could see them making cakes and crumpets. If we had a few coppers we'd buy some for a hap'ney, then tuck into them in the waiting room. After an hour or so, Mr Young would send us on our way in case our mam's worried about us."

Not long afterwards, Pat, June Burns (a cousin who lived at Violet Street) and Joan left South Benwell School. Pat started work at the cheque office at the Co-op: "It was a good job in those days. Each morning I met up with June on our way to work. We would meet at School Street, she lived at the bottom of Violet Street and I lived in the middle of the block. We would walk along and cut down Clara Street for the bus and hang about until Dougie and Steve in the station box noticed us and waved. One morning we were a bit late, it was deep with snow. As we were running down the street, we both slipped, flying through the air and crashed to the ground. When we got up we could see Dougie and Steve laughing their heads off from the signal box. We were dead embarrassed and for weeks we wouldn't go that way for the bus."

June, Joan and Pat were Black Angels, the name given to the girlfriends of teddy boys: "We were the height of fashion, we wore long military macs tied tightly around the waist – mine was green – with black three quarter length drain pipe trousers, little white socks, black ballerina canvas shoes and velvet chokers around our necks. We used to decorate the chokers ourselves with sequins. We were the bees knees. We all wore our hair in the DA cut (which was duck's bum) all short and swept back to a point at the back. The style was also known as the Doris Day cut. We wore big button ear rings to match our poppet necklaces and bracelets. Being Black Angels, we wore giant black ones, they just snapped together, they were great."

Pat Owens wearing her trendy mac. She was a Black Angel, the name given to a girlfriend of a Teddy Boy. The traditional dress of the girls was a black patent leather mac, a choker decorated with sequins, large black beads and ballet style shoes.

A Geordie Life
by Winifred Jackson (née Cockburn)

Winifred Cockburn (pronounced Coburn) was born on 5th October 1937 in Sutton Dwellings, the second eldest of four daughters. She was known locally as Winnie Cockburn which she hated with a passion. She attended Atkinson Road Primary, Junior and Senior school from 1942-1952.

"My Grandfather, Thomas Cockburn was quite a local celebrity being world 100 yards sprint champion who as a professional world sprint champion, won the one hundred pounds Christmas Handicap at the old Victoria running grounds in Newcastle in 1892. As reigning champion, he threw out a challenge, offering any opponent a ten yard start, promising to give one hundred pounds to anyone who could beat him. However, I believe that he remained unbeaten until he finally retired. He was also a proficient boxer, and won the National Coal Board British Boxing Middleweight Championship, so being a famous sporting celebrity in the area, he had the honour of being chosen to be the starter of the very last Blaydon Races in 1916.

Wyn's grandfather Thomas was a boxer and also was the starter for the last Blaydon Races in 1916.

"My father, Ben was also, in his younger days, a professional boxer, having seventeen bouts winning sixteen by knockouts."

Her first job after leaving school was in a solicitor's office, Griffith & Co at the Royal Arcade in Pilgrim Street (Royal Arcade now sadly demolished).

"I met my husband Ron Jackson when I was seventeen. Ron was on his demob leave after serving three years in the Royal and Electrical Mechanical Engineers. We were married in St James' Church when I was eighteen. We lived in a horrible downstairs flat in Beech Street, with a yard and an outside toilet shared with three other families. We were rehoused by the council to Chepstow Road, Denton Burn, where we saved the deposit to buy a house, which was in a lovely cul-de-sac in the old village of Kenton Bank Foot.

"Ron had been a local champion amateur boxer before going into the army, then resumed his boxing career as a professional after we married. He was very successful and fought the British Welterweight Champion in 1959, was ahead on points when he sustained a very badly cut eye, so the referee stopped the fight. Ron started several businesses over the years, the last being

Wyn is standing at the front wearing a dark jacket, white apron and scarf around her neck. The victory tea party was held in Sutton Dwellings in 1945.

the most successful, was as a plastering contractor, Whickham Plastering Co.

"We bought a dilapidated mill with three acres of land at Kirkley Ponteland and, after renovating, we moved in 1975. Our two daughters Yvonne and Michelle stayed with family until we made it habitable.

"In 1982 Ron built Boarding Kennels and Cattery for me to run. We ran the two businesses for the next twenty years before retiring. We bought a bungalow in Darras Hall Ponteland and moved in on 2nd November 2001.

After being so busy and active, I was so bored, I decided to write Ron's life story:

Geordie Got Physical – this book follows Ron from birth to retirement.

Geordie Dropped In – covers his army career.

Ron Jackson became Northumberland champion, he is seen in this photo wearing his gloves and satin shorts.

An extract from *Geordie Got Physical* by Wyn Jackson

Now, when in pensive mood, I reminisce about the "innocent adventures" we experienced as boys, such as the instance when one of our school teachers was reading out aloud to the whole class, the classic story of Tom Sawyer and Huckleberry Finn. We would be about ten years old at the time and the story enthralled us. We sat listening intently to their adventurous escapades, which put ideas into our heads. After school, Alan and I, together with another three boys from our class, devised a plan, which was to creep out of our respective beds that night, while our parents were asleep and to congregate at the top of our back lane at midnight.

From there, the five of us quietly crept the mile to the local cemetery, St James' Churchyard. I recall the night in question was particularly spooky, the sky hung with low heavy clouds, which entirely obscured the stars and moon, resulting in an eerie purplish darkness. To make matters worse it was particularly windy.

Trying to sport brave faces, but feeling anything but, the bunch of us carefully crept into the grave yard, each one trying to panic the other secretly throwing small pebbles and whispering, "What's that?" or asking, "Did you hear that?"

However, we only managed to scare ourselves.

We wandered through the cemetery, gingerly, picking our way past headstones and monuments. The trees were swaying and rustling noisily in the howling wind, their branches creaking and bending almost to breaking point, leaves were scuttling around our feet as our imaginations went into overdrive. We were all truly petrified but would not admit it. All of a sudden Alan pointed and shouted, "Look."

To our horror, we saw a white shape, which appeared to be floating towards us; we were riveted to the spot with fear.

"It's a ghost." Alan whispered.

With that, we spun around and took to our heels, running as if our lives depended on it. We made a beeline for the small stone wall surrounding the graveyard, which was about two feet high and physically threw ourselves over. However, we were traumatised to find ourselves falling from a height of about six feet; unbeknown to us, the ground was at a much lower level on the other side. Consequently, we ended up in a heap, falling one on top of the other; fortunately for us, a small mound of sand helped to soften our fall. We picked ourselves up, and as we dusted ourselves down, we glanced up and to our alarm; the "ghost" appeared at the top of the wall. We were trembling with alarm, when the hazy white form leaped at us. It was only then that we realised it was a large white dog.

An Inspiration for the Younger Generation

by Sylvia Wood (née Kirk)

"One of my earliest memories of Benwell is watching the tar bubbling up on the road on a hot day. It was all gooey and I made a big ball of it which I rolled in my hand. We lived at 93 Maria Street and my gran, my dad's mother, lived at 76 Maughan Street. My gran came to the door and said: 'Oh, if your mother catches you, you'll be in trouble!'

Sylvia remembered being taken indoors by her gran and she rubbed butter into her hands to remove the stains. When they played games in the streets, Sylvia and her friends enjoyed holding on to the bars which were barriers outside the shops, then swing right around them. Her gran had a saying which Sylvia was never quite sure what it meant.

"My granny would say: "There they go crowping their creels."

One of the pass times that Sylvia enjoyed was using a chalk pipe and she mixed soap flakes in a cup with water and blew bubbles. And she was forever in trouble with her mother for pinching the washing line from the back yard to use as a swing. "We strapped it around a street light and hurled ourselves around."

Nellie Peddie, Sylvia's grandmother, who worked as a cleaner at the RVI, this was a typical uniform at the time.

A phrase which was familiar to Sylvia was: "Get down or I'll tell your mam!"

"I remember sliding on one side of our lane between Maria Street and Maughan Street. Their side was concrete and ours was a kind of pink and yellow sand stone. I went on their side especially in the snow. I used a small metal shovel with a handle to ride on. First I had to put candle grease on it but the first time I travelled on it, I didn't get very far – the metal got hot and I burned my backside. So, after that I put a cushion on top. There were huge grooves in the cobbles where a horse and cart used to go. It was difficult to use a sledge there as there was a turning at the bottom, so far down Maria Street."

Sylvia's mam, Lily, and dad, David, met while working at Vickers Armstrong's works in munitions. He later went to the Durham Light Infantry in India and when he came back he worked on the buses, then became an inspector – first on the trams, next the trolley buses and finally on petrol run vehicles. She can remember clearly that her mother had many friends, they were members of the ladies' darts team at the Hydraulic Crane pub on Scotswood Road. Her dad was always taking photographs and there are many taken of the fundraising events and competitions. Her parents went on trips from the Old Hall Social Club and the ladies from the darts team were featured in a programme for Tyne Tees Television during their Easter Bonnet Parade. The women wore handmade hats and their photographs were taken on the roof of the TV studio.

"At the end of the night, they would all walk home together up the steep street, then they'd be outside our front door chatting for ages. My mam would say 'Come on, you can all come in.' They'd all go booling along the passage of our house, go into the sitting room, push all of the furniture back, roll up the carpet, then the music would go on and they'd dance. They'd say 'This is a well sprung floor this one.'

"My uncle Tomma would come to the door the next day, the key was always left on string behind the door. He'd say: 'Yous'll aal be killed in yar beds.'

Friends of the family included Albin and Doreen Myers and their son Geoffrey. The Myers had a shop at the bottom of Frank Street and Geoffrey went to South Benwell School. They sold sweets, newspapers, cigarettes, bread and general supplies.

"He had to be up at six in the morning for the papers for the men on their way to work, it was hard for him to make much of it. Doreen preferred to keep her own job in an office and didn't have the time to help out in the shop. Then Albin went back to his previous profession as a barber. They used to call him Dapper Dan, he had this little wispy tash.

The Hydraulic Crane pub where the ladies darts team met and held their many competitions and fund raising events.

"There used to be dozens of street gangs, and they all met at different places, usually at the corners of the streets, anywhere that we could lean. Dances were held in the church hall of St Aidan's, not discos back then, and no music centres – you had to have a partner. We had a record player which stacked eight records high and they dropped one at a time. There was also a dance on a Wednesday nights. We went to the bottom of Atkinson Road and near the Scotswood Bridge, we were about thirteen or fourteen and we learned how to waltz."

Sylvia was married at St Aidan's Church on Glue House Lane on October 5th 1960. She can picture the appearance of the building and remembered it as having a huge hall with a stage at one end and a billiard table at the other. Sylvia said that it was customary to have a 'Hoy oot' – the wedding couple throwing money from the car to waiting children in the street. There were dances held in the hall.

Aunt Lydia, Ginny Brannen, holding the cup, and Lily Kirk – proud members of the ladies' darts team.

"My dress was made from Nottingham lace, I bought it from Paige's on Northumberland Street. The sleeves went down to a point at the cuff and the back of the dress also went down in a V shape, with a huge voile bow at the back. It was a ballerina style with a huge petticoat, but the dress was so heavy that it needed two more petticoats to make it stand out properly, which I made myself. I had yellow tea roses in the bouquet. My shoes had high heels and were white shiny leather. But I was disappointed with my hairstyle, the hairdresser must have only known one style, and I came out looking like all the old women in my family who were there at the same time. My veil was fitted to appear full and bouncy, then it rained and it was as flat as a pancake."

Sylvia Kirk wearing her organza lace ballerina style wedding dress outside the door of St Aidan's Church.

Sylvia speaks of the day that she received the keys for her first flat in Clara Street: "After I'd picked up the keys, I went to the number 1 bus stop with my friend Shirley Nicholson. In those days we didn't have a telephone, so we were going to Wallsend, to Essex Gardens to tell my mother-in-law the good news. We moved house from 6 Clara Street because we needed more space and that took us to Sutton Dwellings. We also lived at Maughan Street and Ventnor Avenue."

Her working life consisted of firstly working in Bainbridges Wholesale Department, she was there for three years, then at the Newcastle General Hospital as an auxiliary and then moved on to work in the laundry at Walkergate, only leaving there when her daughter, Linda, was born. Sylvia also went to the wash house at Bond Street as a customer and used the swimming pool there.

"The laundry room at Bond Street was just as big as the pool. As you came in the front door, there were swimmers on one side, on the other, big sliding units like a huge wardrobe with hot air circulating – the washers were enormous too."

Sylvia still lives in Benwell in Adelaide House. She has fabulous views of old

Sylvia waiting for the number 1 bus to Wallsend to tell her mother in law the good news that she was the proud owner of a key to a new flat. Not many people owned telephones back then and mobiles would have been thought of as something from a James Bond novel.

Benwell alongside the new buildings to the north up to the West Road and to the west taking in the new Library, old Carnegie Library, St Joseph's Church, St James' Church and the parts of Ethel, Clara, Gerald Street and many more. One of her friends Irene Lucas also lives in the block, but has views south and east. She can see where the old Sutton Dwellings used to be that have now been replaced with two storey, new style housing, and also the Autoparts building, which in the past had been Woolworths, and before that the Adelaide Cinema. Irene has views of Hugh Gardens, Maria Street, St John's Road and as far as the Dunston Rocket, the Gateshead Angel and beyond.

Linda Wood with her new doll's pram in Sutton Dwellings.

The streets of Benwell have continued to influence Sylvia in her creative projects. She runs the craft class at Knit and Natter in the Cornerstone building on Armstrong Road and was also involved in the Woolly West Project.

Judith Green of Northumbria University said: "The Woolly West project covered Benwell and Scotswood. The idea was to rebuild the area in wool, in view of the extensive clearance and redevelopment experienced over the years and especially recently. People were asked to choose buildings or scenes that were important to them – some still remain, and some are long gone. More than 50 people participated – from four main groups – the Cornerstone Knit and Natter group, the Benwell Hall Drive Knit and Natter group, St Margaret's Church (Scotswood), and the Pendower Good Neighbour Project – plus individuals. The buildings and scenes featured in a film called *Knitting Together* made by a local film-maker in collaboration with Search, which was shown on the Community Channel."

A display of the Woolly West at the West End Library. A DVD was compiled about the Woolly West, which includes interview material about the buildings and scenes in it, the making of the film, and information about people's lives.

The Woolly West exhibition has been on display at the West End Library in Condercum Road and was shown at The Biscuit Factory from March to May 2009. Sylvia is proud of the project which shows Vickers complete with tanks, the Green Tree pub, rag and bone man, post boxes, telephone boxes and many more landmarks familiar to the folks from Benwell. Two other women who were involved in projects such as knitted bags which were on display in John Lewis window were Dot Tweddell and Vera Carter of Condercum Court knitting group.

Sylvia's home is an artist's grotto, the place is decorated with her exquisite embroideries, charcoal drawings, pastel work, oil paintings and tablecloths, runners, pillowcases and bedding apart from the clothes that she has designed and made over the years. They are famous in the area. The animated film by Julie Ballands is well worth viewing. Parts of the film were made showing Sylvia, Irene Lucas and Dorothy O'Shea sitting on the decking on the landing over the pond in Benwell Nature Park with their knitting needles.

"We also went to a street that was derelict, it was so overgrown you could hardly see the steps leading up to the house. Julie chose the spots to shoot the film. We got some funny looks – two of us sitting knitting in the street. She put lots of time into the work, especially the part showing how the flowers were growing."

People who have also been involved with the project were women and girls at the Pendower Good neighbour Project who created the views of the city in felting. A cross stitch model of St Margaret's Church was completed by church goers.

Sylvia also enjoys learning new skills at her art class which is run at Lilia Community Centre on Benwell Lane which was run by Niki Black (now by Steve Lyon-Bowes). Sylvia said: "The centre was given the name because it is on the site where a lily pond used to be. I have learned so many skills from Niki. I put a box in the search office for people to donate buttons, we got millions and it took ages to sort out all the black, blue and white ones. They were intended for the children's group at Lilia to make a mosaic of the lily pond."

Sylvia and her group take full advantage of what the Search Project has to offer. There are computer classes, advice desk to help older people to claim their full entitlement of benefits and pensions etc, community health. Local people, who are 50 plus, can learn how to use a digital camera, how to swim, courses on aromatherapy, workshops with everything from how to make a proggy mat to problems experienced by older people using local bus services. She speaks with enthusiasm: "We've taken advantage of the Tai Chi, massage, storytelling events, which always have a moral attached, and in the summer we head for the hills, going to Redcar, Seahouses, Alnwick Castle and Cragside among other places."

It's good to see that so much is still going on in Benwell, the community spirit is still going strong and so long as there are local people working hard to inspire the residents, they can't help but instill a sense of pride in the area for the younger generations.

Three of Sylvia's drawings which she created at the Lilia Centre in Niki Black's group.

Days To Remember

A bus trip from the Delaval Estate in 1950. The crowd are all wearing their best bib and tuckers.

A trip to the seaside. Elsie Moore to the left in the dark suit, Teddy Loughlin wearing a check shirt and Peter Moore leaning forwards in the sand. Gracie Robinson of Hannah Street can be seen looking towards the camera in the background wearing a white dress.

A charabanc trip in Amelia Street back lane. Pat Horsefield's Uncle Robbie is at the wheel ready to take the trippers on a day out. Robbie lived at No 5 Amelia Street with Pat's Auntie Joan. He had also worked as a trolley bus driver and fireman.

Above: The Funeral procession of men from the Montagu Pit Disaster in 1925 passes along Adelaide Terrace. The funerals of major pit disasters always drew large crowds who wanted to pay their respects. Note the people on the ledges of the shops.

Thirty-eight lives were lost in the disaster. The men were trapped underground with no hope of escape and their relatives anxiously waited at the pit head.

Left: Women waiting for news at the pit head of Montagu Pit in 1925.

A victory tea party of 1945 held in the Maria Street and Maughan Street back lane. Sid Abbott can be seen to the far right wearing his waistcoat. Audrey Jacques is the girl third right from the front wearing a flowered dress and white collar. This photo shows mainly children.

Victory tea party of 1945 in the lane of Maria Street and Maughan Street. Agnes Jacques is wearing a short sleeved button front dress at the front of the photo to the far right with son Robert sporting his mop of curly hair. The women are giving the V for Victory sign.

South Benwell School Yard in the early fifties. John Cross can be seen in his braces and white shirt leaning his head to one side to see the photographer. Mary Larkham is standing at the back of the yard with long hair and wearing a lighter coat. Notice the drummer boys.

Acknowledgements

I would like to thank all of the people who gave up their time to tell me their stories, trusted me to borrow their photos to scan and allowed me to place copies of them in the West Newcastle Picture History Collection which is based at the West End Library Condercum Road. Special thanks to Fred Millican, Mike Young, Linda Sutton and Harry Bennett, members of the group who have become invaluable to me during my research. And Des Walton who helped to set up the group from the beginning. Also thanks to Ian Whillis and Terry Quinn for their wonderful photographs.

Staff at the West End Library who have encouraged me, Christine Wood, Margaret Donkin, and to Heri and Patrick, who are always at hand with a smile, to put out resources for our group. Also to Sheila Naughton and Mary Butler, Senior Library and Information Officers for their support and for including me in workshops and local events.

To the Search Project on Adelaide Terrace and Judith Green who are always there to provide illusive information. Les Turnbull and Alan Thompson who gave me assistance at the Miners' Institute by pointing me in the right direction and Miners' Institute staff who copied maps and mining information. George Nairn for his old postcards.

Yvonne Young in her role as Florrie the Geordie Housewife – writer and poet. Yvonne performs her poetry throughout Tyneside.

Peter Moore, who has listened, gave advice and provided photos for me to use, although he has written his own book and may need them for that.

Andrew Clark for having faith in me to go ahead with this project and the help and support that I have received throughout.

Jimmy Forsyth for the inspiration to match up photos with stories and Sandra Smith from his care home for giving me the time to spend with Jimmy.

And most of all to the people of Benwell who still live and work in the area, for allowing me to take their photographs and for their patience when I was pestering them during their busy working days by asking questions, hats off to all.

Also available from Summerhill Books

All the Lads & Lasses
Memories of Childhood in West Newcastle